Nathan Boughton Warren

The Holidays

Christmas, Easter, and Whitsuntide; together with the May-day, Midsummer, and

harvest-home festivals

Nathan Boughton Warren

The Holidays
Christmas, Easter, and Whitsuntide; together with the May-day, Midsummer, and harvest-home festivals

ISBN/EAN: 9783337289485

Printed in Europe, USA, Canada, Australia, Japan

Cover: Foto ©Andreas Hilbeck / pixelio.de

More available books at **www.hansebooks.com**

THE HOLIDAYS:

Christmas, Easter, and Whitsuntide;

TOGETHER WITH THE

MAY-DAY, MIDSUMMER, AND HARVEST-HOME FESTIVALS.

BY

NATHAN B. W█████N.

ILLUSTRATED BY F.█

"I like them well—the curio█
And all pretended gravity █
That seek to banish hence█
Have thrust away much a█

█ay Book.

THIRD █

█H

CONTENTS.

APPENDIX.

ILLUSTRATIONS.

CHAPTER I.

REG-
ORY
the
Great
appears to be chief
among the originators
of the social festivities
which, since his time,
have distinguished the
celebration of the
Christmas Holidays. In
a letter to Mellitus, a
British Abbot (after-
wards a successor of
Augustine in the See
of Canterbury), he says:
"Whereas the people
were accustomed to sac-
rifice many oxen in
honor of demons, let

them celebrate a religious and solemn festival and not slay the animals, ' *diabolo* ' — ' to the devil,' but to be eaten by themselves ' *ad laudem Dei* ' — ' to the praise of God.' "

In an earlier age, a very similar course had facilitated the conversion to Christianity of the populous district of Neo-Cæsarea in Pontus. Gregory, Bishop of that Diocese, is said to have changed the observance of the Pagan festivals to those of the Christian saints and martyrs, retaining such of their ancient festivities and ceremonies as were in themselves harmless, and to which the people were greatly attached.

But adaptations such as these were not made without exciting serious apprehensions, for Gregory Nazianzen and other Fathers of the Church, like the Puritans of modern times, warned their flocks against these secularizing tendencies, and the danger of excess in feasting, dancing, crowning the doors, and similar festive practices. They feared that these things would carry their people back into Paganism or Judaism.

Gregory the Great, however, does not appear to have been troubled by any such scruples, for, as we have seen, he recommended to the Anglo-Saxon missionaries a more liberal course in regard to social festivities.

Gregory, or as he is called in the English Calendar, St. Gregory, was of noble family and devoted from his earliest youth to religion and learning, giving all his estate to the building and maintaining of religious houses. He, therefore, could not be called worldly-

minded, nor taking into account his extensive mission-
ary operations, could he be accused of being lacking in
evangelical zeal.

A rare tract of 1648 thus quaintly alludes to Gregory's letter : —

" If it doth appeare that the time of this festival doth comply with
the time of the Heathen's *Saturnalia*, this leaves no charge of impiety upon it, for since things are best cured by their contraries, it
was both wisdom and piety in the ancient Christians (whose work
it was to convert the Heathens from such, as well as other superstitions and miscarriages), to vindicate such times from the service
of the Devil, by appoynting them to the more solemne and especiall
service of God."

The Roman missionaries derived no inconsiderable
assistance from the Calendar they found already in existence among their heathen converts. For the great
Pagan festivals of the ancient world were regulated by
the sun, their Feast of Yule, or " Juul," being about the
winter solstice, or Christmas ; the Festival of Eoster,
or Easter, about the vernal equinox ; and that of Midsummer, or St. John Baptist's Day, at the summer solstice. These most ancient of the world's festivals,
under changed names and with new objects, are still
kept in our own times.

We are not, however, to infer, as many archæologists
have done, that the social festivities of the Christian
holidays are altogether of heathen origin ; on the contrary they may claim for themselves a much higher
authority. In fact, our Christmas, Easter, and Whitsun

festivals have taken the place of the three great feasts of the Jewish Church, — the feasts of Passover, of Weeks, and of Tabernacles.

In the social festivities of the most joyous of these festivals, the Feast of Tabernacles, there is a striking resemblance to those of the Christmas holidays.

The requirements of The Law with respect to this festival were: —

"And thou shalt rejoice in thy feast, thou, and thy son, and thy daughter, and thy manservant, and thy maidservant, and the Levite, the stranger, and the fatherless, and the widow, that are within thy gates. Seven days shalt thou keep a solemn feast unto the Lord thy God in the place which the Lord shall choose: because the Lord thy God shall bless thee in all thine increase, and in all the works of thine hands, therefore thou shalt surely rejoice." — *Deut.* xvi. 14, 15.

Smith, in his " Dictionary of the Bible," gives an interesting account of the manner in which this injunction of Moses was observed in after-times by the Jews in Jerusalem. He says: —

"Though all the Hebrew Annual Festivals were seasons of rejoicing, the Feast of Tabernacles was in this respect distinguished above them all. The huts and the *lûlâbs* must have made a gay and striking spectacle over the city by day ; and the lamps, the flambeaux, the music, and the joyous gatherings in the court of the Temple, must have given a still more festive character to the night. .... At the Temple in the evening (after the day with which the festivals had commenced, had ended), both men and women assembled in the Court of the Women, expressly to hold a rejoicing for the drawing of the water of Siloam. On this occasion a degree of unrestrained hilarity was permitted, such as would have been unbecoming while the ceremony itself was going on, in the presence of the Altar, and in connection with the offering of the Morning Sacrifice. . . . . At the same time there were set up in the Court two lofty stands, each supporting four great lamps. These were lighted on each night of the Festival ; and, as it is said, they cast their light over nearly the whole compass of the city. Many in the assembly carried flambeaux ; a body of Levites stationed on the fifteen steps leading up to the Women's Court, played instruments of music and chanted the fifteen psalms (120 to 134), which are called in the A. V. 'Songs of Degrees.' Singing and dancing were afterwards continued for some time ; the same ceremonies in the day, and the same joyous meetings in the evening, were renewed on each of the seven days."

The severity of our Puritanical forefathers who imagined that the social festivities of their times were merely "heathenish vanities," is only equaled by their misconception in regard to the character of the Jewish holidays.

The learned, to the confusion of Judaizing zealots of the Puritanical school, have clearly established the fact that the Jewish Festivals were, even in the time of our Saviour and his Apostles, seasons of general social enjoyment. In conformity with the positive injunctions of the Mosaic Law, the New Moons, the Passover, the Feast of Pentecost and of Tabernacles, were observed with a degree of hilarity altogether inconsistent with the modern Puritanical notions of propriety. Indeed, they applied very literally the words of the Psalmist, " Serve the Lord with gladness, and come before his presence with a song."

According to Bishop Horne and other Biblical

scholars, the greatness of these rejoicings and their happening at the time of the vintage led Tacitus to suppose that the Jews were accustomed to sacrifice to Bacchus.

The joyous nature of these festivals has been briefly but forcibly depicted by the author of "Festivals, Games, and Amusements."

"The sacred ceremonies which, exclusive of the pomp of sacrifice, the perfume of rich odors, and a stately display of gorgeously attired processionists in the courts of their venerated temple, and in the presence of a whole assembled people, combined the attractions of male and female dancers with all the enchantments of the most exquisite musicians and singers, were not only incomparably more grand, imposing, and magnificent, as a mere spectacle, than any theatrical exhibition that the world could produce, but appealed to the heart while they delighted the eye ; gratified the soul as well as the sense ; awakened feelings of patriotism as well as religion, and by uniting the splendors of earth to the glorious hopes of heaven, constituted a union of fascinations which no sensitive or pious Jew could have contemplated without an ecstasy of delight."

As our Saviour went up regularly to these feasts at Jerusalem, and as the Apostles also continued even after the Ascension and the outpouring of the Spirit on the Day of Pentecost, to take part in these national festivals, we may, therefore, reasonably conclude, that there can be nothing in holiday festivities, inconsistent with the profession of the principles of Christianity.

CHAPTER II.

CHRISTMAS.

H E term Christmas is derived from *Christ* and the Saxon "*maisse*" signifying the Mass, and a Feast.

The religious observance of the festival dates from a period as early, at least, as the second century. Haydn says it was first observed A. D. 98. Clement, the co-worker of St. Paul, mentioned by him in his Epistle to the Philippians (iv. 3), says:

" Brethren, keep diligently feast days; and truly in the first place the day of Christ's birth."

It was ordered to be kept as a solemn Feast, and with the performance of Divine Services, on the 25th of December, by Telesphorus, Bishop of Rome, about A. D. 137. His injunctions are, "that in the holy night of the Nativity of our Lord and Saviour, they do celebrate public Church services, and in them solemnly sing the Angels' Hymn, because also the same night he was declared unto the shepherds by an angel, as the truth itself doth witnesse." In the same age Theophilus, Bishop of Cæsarea, recommends " the celebration of the birth-day of Our Lord, on what day soever the 25th of December shall happen." In the following century, Cyprian begins his "Treatise on the Nativity," thus: " The much wished for and long expected Nativity of Christ is come, the famous solemnity is come."

Gregory Nazianzen and St. Basil both have sermons on this day. St. Chrysostom also says: " This day was of great antiquity, and of long continuance, being famous and renowned in the Church from the beginning, far and wide, from Thrace as far as Gades in Spain." And he styles it, "the most venerable and tremendous of all festivals, and the Metropolis or Mother of all Festivals."

Brady in his " Clavis Calendaria " says : —

" The first Christians, who, it is proper to remark, were all converts from the Hebrews, solemnized the nativity on the first of January, conforming in this computation to the Roman year, though it is to be particularly noticed, that on the day of the Feast of Tabernacles they ornamented their churches with green boughs, as a memorial that Christ was actually born at that time, in like manner as the ancient Jews erected booths or tents which they inhabited at this season, to keep up by an express command from God the remembrance of their deliverance from Egyptian bondage, and of their having dwelt in tents or tabernacles in the wilderness."

Blunt, in his " Annotated Book of Common Prayer," observes : —

" Most of the Fathers have left sermons which were preached on Christmas Day, or during the continuance of the festival. And secular decrees of the Christian emperors, as well as canons of the Church, show, that it was very strictly observed as a time of rest from labour, of Divine Worship, and of Christian hilarity, and that 'it is most fit that the season so marked out by angels by songs of joy such as had not been heard on Earth since the Creation, should also be observed as a time of festive gladness by the Church, and in the social life of Christians."

This festive gladness has always been a marked feature in an English Christmas. The enthusiasm with which its arrival is announced is thus felicitously expressed by Thomas Millar : —

" The hundreds of silver-toned bells of London ring loud, deep, and clear, from tower and spire, to welcome in Christmas. The far-stretching suburbs, like glad children, take up and fling back the sound over hill and valley, marsh and meadow, while steeple calls to steeple across the winding arms of the mast-crowded river, proclaiming to the heathen voyager who has brought his treasures to our coast, and who is ignorant of our religion, the approach of some great Christian festival."

The towns of England have been described by Stowe and other old writers as presenting at this season a sylvan appearance; the houses dressed with branches of ivy and holly; the churches converted into leafy tabernacles, and standards bedecked with evergreens set up in the streets, while the young of both sexes danced around them.

It is interesting to observe from such descriptions, the close resemblance between these manners and customs, and those described in the passages quoted from Smith and Brady; when, in accordance with Scripture injunctions, the people of Israel went forth into the mount and brought thence " olive-branches, and pine-branches, and myrtle-branches, and palm-branches, and branches of thick trees, and made themselves booths, every one upon the roof of his house, and in their courts, and in the courts of the house of God, and in the street of the water-gate, and in the street of the gate of Ephraim."

" The ancient custom of dressing our churches and houses at Christmas with evergreens, appears to be not only thus traceable to the Feast of Tabernacles, but is also supposed to have been derived from certain expressions in the following prophecies of the coming of our Saviour: 'Behold the days come, saith the Lord, that I will raise unto David a Righteous Branch;' 'For behold I will bring forth my servant the Branch;' 'Thus speaketh the Lord of Hosts, saying, behold the Man whose name is The Branch, and He shall grow up out of his place; 'At that time will I cause the Branch of Righteousness to grow up unto David;' 'Thus saith the Lord God, I will also take of the highest Branch of the High Cedar, and will set it; I will crop off from the top of his young twigs a tender one, and will plant it upon an high mountain and eminent; in the mountain of the height of Israel will I plant it, and it shall bring forth boughs, and bear fruit, and it shall be a goodly Cedar;' 'In

that day shall the Branch of the Lord be beautiful and glorious ; '
' For He shall grow up before Him as a tender plant, and as a root
out of a dry ground ; and the Lord shall reign over them in Mount
Zion from henceforth even for ever ; ' ' There shall come forth a
rod out of the stem of Jesse, and a branch shall grow out of his
roots, which shall stand for an ensign of the people, and my servant
David shall be their Prince for ever.'

" For it must be confessed that those passages and expressions in
which our Saviour is represented under the type of a Branch, a
Righteous Branch, a Bough, the Branch of Righteousness, who will
reign for ever, etc., in the above quoted clear and eminent prophecies of his first appearance in the flesh upon earth, are in a most
lively manner brought to our memories, and unmistakably alluded
to by those *branches* and *boughs* of evergreens, with which our
churches and houses are adorned, whose gay appearance and perpetual verdure, in that dead season of the year, when all Nature
looks comfortless, dark, and dreary, and when the rest of the
vegetable world has shed its honors, does agreeably charm the
unwearied beholder and make a very suitable accompaniment of
the universal joy which always attends the annual commemoration
of that holy festival." — See *Gentleman's Magazine*, 1765.

Another quaint old writer thus spiritualizes the
practice of Christmas decoration : —

" So our churches and houses, decked with bayes and rosemary,
holly and ivy, and other plants which are always green, winter and
summer, signify and put us in mind of His Deity ; that the Child
who now was born was God and Man, who should spring up like a
tender plant, should always be green and flourishing, and live for
evermore."

In this custom there appears to be also a reference
to those passages of the prophet Isaiah, which foretell
the felicities attending the coming of Christ, namely :
" The glory of Lebanon shall come unto thee, the fir-

tree, the pine-tree, and the box, together, to *beautify the place of my sanctuary*." (Isaiah lx. 13.) " Instead of the thorn, shall come up the fir-tree, and instead of the brier shall come up the myrtle-tree, and it shall be to the Lord for a name, for an everlasting sign that shall not be cut off."

CHAPTER III.

CHRISTMAS CAROLS.

AROL singing appears to have originated in a usage of the Primitive Church, for " In the early ages the bishops were accustomed to sing Carols on Christmas Day with their clergy." Jeremy Taylor, referring to this custom in his " Great Exemplar," says of the " *Gloria in Excelsis*,"[1] "As soon as those blessed choristers had sung their *Christmas Carol*, and taught the church a hymn to put into

[1] See Appendix.

her offices for ever in the anniversary of this Festivity, the angels returned into heaven."

The term "carol" is supposed to be derived either from the Italian "caroli"—a song of devotion, or carol, properly "a round dance."[1] Carols, it is said, were early introduced by the clergy into England from Italy, probably soon after the Norman Conquest, as a substitute for the Yule and Wassail songs of heathen origin, which, until then, had been in use among the vulgar. The custom of singing these "caroli" is still maintained in Italy; indeed, on the continent, caroling at Christmas is almost universal, and particularly in Rome, where, during the season of Advent, the Pifferari may be seen and heard performing their Novena before the shrine of the Madonna and Bambino. These pilgrims, who, by the way, are

---

[1] French *carole, querole;* Breton *keroll,* a dance ; Welsh *coroli,* to reel, to dance.

> " Tho mightest thou karollis sene
> And folke dance and merie ben,
> And made many a faire tourning
> Upon the green grass springing."
>
> *Romaunt of the Rose,* A. D. 760.

Chanson de carole, a song accompanying a dance ; then, as French *balade,* from Italian *ballare,* to dance, applied to the song itself. Diez suggests *chorulus,* from *chorus,* as the origin. But we have no occasion to invent a diminutive, as the Latin *corolla,* from *corona,* gives the exact sense required. Robert of Brune calls the circuit of Druidical stones a carol."

> " The Bretons ranged about the felde
> The *karole* of the stones behelde,
> Many tyme yede tham about,
> Biheld within, biheld without."
>
> *Wedgwood's Dictionary.*

shepherds from the Calabrian Mountains, annually flock to Rome at this season. Their picturesque costume is thus described in " Roba di Roma : " —

" On their heads they wear conical felt hats adorned with a frayed peacock's feather, or a faded band of red cords and tassels ; their bodies are clad in red waistcoats, blue jackets, and small-clothes of skin or yellowish homespun cloth ; skin sandals are bound to their feet with cords that interlace each other up the leg as far as the knee, — and over all is worn a long brown or blue cloak with a short cape, buckled closely round the neck. Sometimes, but rarely, this cloak is of a deep red with a scalloped cape. As they stand before the pictures of the Madonna, their hats placed on the ground before them, and their thick disheveled hair covering their sunburnt brows, blowing away on their instruments or pausing to sing their *novena*, they form a picture which every artist desires to paint. These Pifferari always go in couples, one playing on the zampogna or bagpipe, the base and treble accompaniment, and the other on the piffero, or pastoral pipe, which carries the air. Sometimes one of them varies the performance by singing, in a strong peasant voice, verse after verse of the *novena* to the accompaniment of the bagpipe."

But to return from this digression. The old English Yule songs before referred to, are mentioned by Brady in his " Calendaria " (1808). He says that in his time they were still sung by the people about the church-yards after service on Christmas Day. The example given by him is identical with that in the Christmas of Washington Irving's " Sketch Book."

> " Ule, Ule, Ule, Ule,
> Three puddings in a pule,
> Crack nuts and cry Ule."

These Yule songs, it appears, were sung at the bringing in of the Christmas block, or Yule-log, which was anciently introduced into the old English baronial hall with much pomp and circumstance, the minstrels saluting its appearance with a song. The following specimen from the Sloane MS. is supposed to be of the time of Henry VI., and appears to have been a sort of intermediate link between the ancient Yule song and its more orthodox substitute, the Christmas Carol.

WELCOME YULE!

" Welcome be thou heavenly King,
Welcome, born on this morning,
Welcome for whom we shall sing,
Welcome Yule !

" Welcome be ye Stephen and John,
Welcome Innocents every one,
Welcome Thomas, Martyr-one,
Welcome Yule !

" Welcome be ye, good New Year,
Welcome Twelfth-Day, both in fere,
Welcome Saints, loved and dear,
Welcome Yule !

" Welcome be ye, Candlemas,
Welcome be ye Queen of Bliss,
Welcome both to more and less,
Welcome Yule !

"Welcome be ye that are here,
Welcome all, and make good cheer,
Welcome all another year,
Welcome Yule!"

The Carol for St. Stephen's Day, which follows this, founded on an ancient legend, is of the beginning of the fourteenth century. Very nearly the original words are given as a specimen of the language of the period. In the carol entitled "The Carnal and the Crane," this same legend appears in a more modern dress.

CAROL FOR ST. STEPHEN'S DAY.

"Saint Stephen was a clerk
In King Herode's hall,
And served him of bread and cloth
As ever king befalle.[1]

"Stephen out of kitchen came
With boar's head in hande,
He saw a star was fair and bright,
Over Bethlem stande.

"He cast adown the boar's head,
And went into the halle:—
'I forsake thee, King Herod,
And thy werkes alle.

"'I forsake thee, King Herod,
And thine werkes alle,
There is a child in Bethlem borne,
Is better than we alle.'

---

[1] Befalle, *i. e.*, happened; — as well as ever happened to a king.

2

' ' What aileth thee, Stephen,
    What is thee befalle?
    Lacketh thee either meat or drink,
    In King Herod's hall?'

" ' Lacketh me neither meat nor drink
    In King Herod's hall,
    There is a child in Bethlem borne,
    Is better than we all.'

" ' What aileth thee, Stephen,
    Art thou wode.[1] or thou ginnest to brede?[2]
    Lacketh thee either gold or fee,
    Or any rich weede?'[3]

" ' Lacketh me neither gold nor fee,
    Nor none rich weede,
    There is a child in Bethlem borne
    Shall help us at our need.'

" ' That is all so sooth, Stephen,
    All so sooth, I wiss,
    As this capon crow shall,
    That lyeth here in my dish.'

" That word was not so soon said,
    That word in that hall,
    The capon crew, ' *Christus natus est,*'
    Among the lordes alle.

---

[1] Wode, *i. e.*, mad.

[2] Brede, *i. e.*, upbraid. Danish, "bebreide." In Chaucer the line, — "For veray wo out of his wit he braide," is explained, " He went, or ran out of his wits."

[3] Weede, *i. e.*, dress.

" Riseth up my tormentors,
　　By two, and all by one,
　　And leadeth Stephen out of town,
　　And stoneth him with stone.

" Token they Stephen,
　　And stoned him in the way,
　　And therefore is his even,
　　On Christe's owen day."

The custom of carol singing formerly prevailed over the greater part of the British Isles, and there are still in use in many places, especially among the peasantry of Derbyshire and Lancashire, Yorkshire, Northumberland, and Durham, carols of undoubted antiquity, illustrative of the manners and sentiments of the Middle Ages, some of which are said to be fragments of the Mystery and Miracle Plays, formerly enacted at this season. The following are selected as specimens from these curious old carols : —

AS JOSEPH WAS A-WALKING.[1]

" As Joseph was a-walking,
　　He heard an angel sing,
' This night shall be the birth-time
　　Of Christ the Heav'nly King.

" ' He neither shall be born
　　In housen nor in hall,
　　Nor in the place of Paradise,
　　But in an ox's stall.

---

[1] For music see Appendix.

" ' He neither shall be clothed
    In purple nor in pall,
  But in the fair white linen
    That usen babies all.

" ' He neither shall be rocked
    In silver nor in gold,
  But in a wooden manger
    That resteth on the mould.'

" As Joseph was a-walking,
    There did an angel sing ;
  And Mary's child at midnight
    Was born to be our king.

" Then be ye glad good people,
    This night of all the year,
  And light ye up your candles,
    For His star it shineth clear."

The next specimen seems to have been founded on a legend from one of the Apocryphal Gospels. It exhibits, says Mr. Howitt, a striking impress of the character of the Middle Ages, and shows how well they understood the true spirit of Christ. The music is to be found in the Appendix : —

THE HOLY WELL.

" Honor the leaves, and the leaves of life
    Upon this blest holiday,
  When Jesus asked his mother dear
    Whether He might go to play.

"'To play! to play!' said Blessed Mary,
'To play, then, get you gone;
And see there be no complaint of you
At night when you come home.'

"Sweet Jesus He ran into yonder town
As far as the Holy Well;
And there He saw three as fine children
As ever eyes beheld.

"He said, 'God bless you every one,
And sweet may your sleep be;
And now, little children, I'll play with you,
And you shall play with Me.'

"'Nay, nay, we are Lords' and Ladies' sons —
Thou art meaner than us all;
Thou art but a silly fair maid's child
Born in an oxen's stall."

"Sweet Jesus turned Him around,
And He neither laugh'd nor smiled,
But the tears came trickling from his eyes,
Like water from the skies.

"Sweet Jesus He ran to his mother dear,
As fast as He could run —
'O mother, I saw three as fine children
As ever were eyes set on.

"'I said, "God bless you every one,
And sweet may your sleep be;
And now, little children, I'll play with you,
And you shall play with Me.'

"'"Nay," said they, "we're Lords' and Ladies' sons,
    Thou art meaner than us all;
For thou art but a poor fair maid's child,
    Born in an oxen's stall."'

"'Though you are but a maiden's child
    Born in an oxen's stall,
Thou art the Christ, the King of Heaven,
    And the Saviour of them all.

"'Sweet Jesus, go down to yonder town,
    As far as the Holy Well,
And take away those sinful souls
    And dip them deep in hell.'

"'Nay, nay,' 'sweet Jesus said,
    'Nay, nay, that may not be,
For there are too many sinful souls
    Crying out for the help of Me.'[1]

"O, then spoke the Angel Gabriel,
    Upon one good Saint Stephen,
'Although you're but a maiden's child,
    You are the King of Heaven.'

Numeral Hymns were common in the olden time.
The following is one of the most ancient of all the
popular carols ; the original, preserved among the
Sloane MSS., and of a date not later than the fourteenth century, is entitled —

---

[1] This response seems to have been suggested by the answer made by
Christ to the disciples when they would have called down fire from heaven. —
Luke ix. 54, 55.

"JOYES FYVE."

" The first good joy our Mary had,
  It was the joy of one,
To see her own Son Jesus
  To suck at her breast bone,
  To suck at her breast bone.
    Good man, and blessed, may he be
      Both Father, Son, and Holy Ghost,
    And Christ to eternity.

" The next good joy our Mary had,
  It was the joy of two,
To see her own Son Jesus
  To make the lame to go ;
  To make the lame to go.
    Good man, etc.

" The next good joy our Mary had,
  It was the joy of three,
To see her own Son Jesus
  To make the blind to see ;
  To make the blind to see.
    Good man, etc.

" The next good joy our Mary had,
  It was the joy of four,
To see her own Son Jesus
  To read the Bible o'er ;
  To read the Bible o'er.
    Good man, etc.

" The next good joy our Mary had,
  It was the joy of five,

To see her own Son Jesus
To raise the dead alive;
To raise the dead alive.
Good man, etc.

"The next good joy our Mary had,
It was the joy of six,
To see her own Son Jesus
To wear the crucifix;
To wear the crucifix.
Good man, etc.

"The next good joy our Mary had,
It was the joy of seven,
To see her own Son Jesus
To wear the crown of Heaven,
To wear the crown of Heaven.
Good man, and blessed may he be,
Both Father, Son, and Holy Ghost,
And Christ to eternity."

The following popular carol is from a Kentish version : —

CHRISTMAS DAY IN THE MORNING.

"I saw three ships come sailing in,
On Christmas Day, on Christmas Day;
I saw three ships come sailing in,
On Christmas Day in the morning.[1]

"And what was in those ships all three? etc. ;
And what was in those ships all three? etc.

[1] In *singing* this carol, repeat after the first line of *each* verse, "On Christmas Day, on Christmas Day," and after the second line, "On Christmas Day in the morning."

" Our Saviour Christ and his ladie, etc. ;
Our Saviour Christ and his ladie, etc.

" Pray whither sailed those ships all three? etc. ;
Pray whither sailed those ships all three? etc.

" O they sailed into Bethlehem, etc. ;
O they sailed into Bethlehem, etc.

" And all the bells on earth shall ring, etc. ;
And all the bells on earth shall ring, etc.

" And all the Angels in Heaven shall sing, etc. ;
And all the Angels in Heaven shall sing, etc.

" And all the Souls on Earth shall sing, etc. ;
And all the Souls on Earth shall sing, etc.

" Then let us all rejoice amain, etc. ;
Then let us all rejoice amain, etc."

Ritson thinks that the different versions of this carol may have had their origin in the following curious fragment found by him in Scotland : —

" There comes a ship far sailing then,
Saint Michel was the stieres-man ;
Saint John sate in the horn :
Our Lord harped, our Lady sang,
And all the bells of heaven they rang,
On Christ's Sonday at morn."

The carol entitled " The Holly and the Ivy," is from Sylvester's collection, and is derived from an old broadside printed more than a century and a half ago. The holly, from time immemorial, has been the favorite Christmas evergreen. Dr. Turner, an early English writer on plants, calls it " holy " and " holy-tree ; " which appellation was given it, most probably, from its being used in holy places. " It has a great variety of names in Germany, amongst which is *Christdorn ;* in Danish it is also called *Christhorn ;* and in Swedish *Christtorn*, amongst other appellations; from whence it appears that it is considered a holy plant, by many people in those countries."

THE HOLLY AND THE IVY.[1]

" The Holly and the Ivy
   Now are both well grown,
Of all the trees that are in the wood,
   The holly bears the crown.
Chorus. — The rising of the sun,
     The running of the deer,
     The playing of the merry organ,
     The singing in the choir.

" The holly bears a blossom
   As white as the lily flower,
And Mary bore sweet Jesus Christ,
   To be our sweet Saviour.
Chorus. — The rising of the sun, etc.

" The holly bears a berry,
   As red as any blood,

[1] Music in the Appendix.

And Mary bore sweet Jesus Christ,
　To do poor sinners good.
Chorus. — The rising of the sun, etc.

" The holly bears a prickle
　As sharp as any thorn,
And Mary bore sweet Jesus Christ,
　On Christmas Day in the morn.
Chorus. — The rising of the sun, etc.

" The holly bears a bark,
　As bitter as any gall,
And Mary bore sweet Jesus Christ,
　For to redeem us all.
Chorus. — The rising of the sun, etc.

" The holly and the ivy
　Now are both well grown,
Of all the trees that are in the wood,
　The holly bears the crown.
Chorus. — The rising of the sun," etc.

So popular had carols such as these become in the fifteenth century, that Wynkyn de Worde, one of the earliest printers, published a collection of them in 1521, containing among others, the celebrated " Boar's Head Carol," the best in the collection ; [1] for besides the devotional carols in use at the season, there were those of a convivial character. These "jolie carols," as old Tusser calls them, were sung by the company or by itinerant minstrels who attended the feasts for the purpose.

---

[1] See Appendix for the music of this famous carol.

"Our early songs and carols have commonly a burthen of two lines at the commencement, and not as
now, at the *end* of the stanza. This burthen was intended to be sung by undervoices throughout the song
to support the tune, as in the Boar's Head Carol.

The Reformation, it appears, did not by any means
impair the popularity of the Christmas Carol in England. Says an old writer of 1631, "Suppose Christmas now approaching, the evergreen ivy trimming and
adorning the portals and partcloses of so frequented a
building; the *usual carols* to observe antiquity cheer-
fully sounding, and that which is the complement of
his inferior comforts, his neighbors, whom he tenders
as members of his own family, join with him in this
consort of mirth and melody."

One of these Christmas Carols, printed about the
same period, recites some of the peculiar *pastimes* of
the season : —

"Hark how the wagges abroad doe call
Each other forthe to rambling;
Anon you 'll see them in the hall
For nuts and apples scrambling ;
The wenches with their wassail bowles
About the streets are singing ;
The boyes are come to catch the owles,
The wild mare is in bringing."

Mr. Davies Gilbert, in his collection of ancient Christmas Carols, says, that in the West of England on
Christmas Day, carols "took the place of psalms in all

the churches, especially at afternoon service, the whole congregation joining; and at the end it was usual for the parish clerk to declare, in a loud voice, his wishes for a merry Christmas and a happy New Year, to all the parishioners."

In Wales, Christmas caroling is still kept up, perhaps to a greater extent even than in England. After the turn of midnight on Christmas Eve, divine service is celebrated, followed by the singing of carols to the harp; and they are also with similar accompaniment sung in the *houses*, during the continuance of the Christmas holidays.

Before the Reformation, the interval between the midnight mass and that at daybreak was passed in singing carols and in peculiar dances, which were shared in by young and old.

This practice of midnight caroling was once very general. Indeed, throughout the whole season of Advent, bands of vocal and instrumental performers made their rounds, charming the wintry nights preceding Christmas with their minstrelsy.

This custom of carol singing at Christmas is one which of late years has greatly revived and become generally popular both in Europe and America. The usage, however, has been made to conform in great measure to our modern notions of propriety and convenience. Itinerant minstrels seldom now awaken people from their slumbers at midnight with the carol

"God rest you merry gentlemen,
Let nothing you dismay!"

Nor do the waits in these days often go from house to house and from hamlet to hamlet, " all the night long chanting such carols as our pious forefathers loved well to listen to."

> "Wake me that I the twelvemonth long,
>   May bear the song
> About me in the world's throng;
> That treasured joys of Christmas tide
> May with mine hour of gloom abide;
>   The Christmas Carol ring
> Deep in my heart, when I would sing,
> Each of the twelve good days,
> Its earnest yield of duteous love and praise,
> Ensuring happy months, and hallowing common ways."
>
> *Keble.*

In days of yore a variety of instruments, beside the harp, were used by the minstrels. Morley, in his " Consort Lessons," dedicated to the Lord Mayor and Aldermen of London, 1529, speaks of the treble and base viols, the flute, the cittern or English guitar, the treble lute, and the pandora.

In more modern times the waits used hautboys of four different sizes.

In ancient times, the chief of the nobility maintained in their households bands of their own, but ordinarily minstrels went about from house to house. In return for the hospitality received, they sang the praises of their noble host, showering down blessings on him and the family.

The Norman Carol, translated by Dr. Douce from a

MS. in the British Museum, presents a pleasing picture of this mediæval custom : —

"Lordlings, listen to our ditty,
Strangers coming from afar;
Let poor minstrels move your pity,
Give us welcome, soothe our care.
In this mansion, as they tell us,
Christmas wassail keeps to-day,
And, as king of all good fellows,
Reigns with uncontrolled sway."

CHAPTER IV.

CHRISTMAS IN THE HALLS OF OLD ENGLAND.

RING-
I N G
in the
Yule-
l o g
a n d
placing it on the
hearth of the wide fire-
place in the hall, was,
in the olden time, one
of the most joyous
of the ceremonies con-
nected with the obser-
vance of the Christ-
mas holidays.

The custom of burn-
ing the Yule-log is said
to have originated with the Danes and Pagan Saxons,
who made bonfires at the winter solstice, or Yule, in

honor of their god Thor, and is supposed to have been emblematic of the return of the sun with its increasing light and warmth. On the introduction of Christian-ity, the illuminations of this Feast of Yule were con-tinued "as representative of that *True Light* which was then ushered into the world in the person of our Saviour, 'the Day-spring from on High.'"

"The venerable Yule-log, destined to crackle a welcome to all comers, was drawn," says Mr. Chambers, "in triumph from its resting place at the feet of its living brethren of the woods. Each wayfarer raised his hat as it passed, for he well knew it was full of good promises, and that its flame would burn out old wrongs and heart-burnings."

In the olden time, the lighting of the Yule-log was the signal for a general cessation of work; and for an energetic devotion to the traditional sports and pastimes of the season.

Vestiges of this custom are to be found even in this country. In Connecticut, at the house of an ancestor of the writer, the size of the Yule-log was a matter of no small importance; for, so long as it burned, all work on the farm was suspended.

In Drake's "Winter Nights," mention is made of the Yule-log, as lying "in ponderous majesty on the kitchen floor," until each had sung his Yule song, "standing on its centre," ere it was consigned to the flames that

"Went roaring up the chimney wide."

A specimen of one of these songs, the carol "Wel-

3

come Yule," is given in the preceding chapter. Herrick
furnishes us with another, which the artist has illustrated in the initial letter : —

> " Come, bring with a noise,
>   My merry, merry boys,
> The Christmas log to the firing ;
>   While my good dame, she
>   Bids ye all be free,
> And drink to your heart's desiring.

> " With the last year's brand
>   Light the new block, and
> For good success in his spending,
>   On your psaltries play,
>   That sweet luck may
> Come while the log is a-teending " (kindling).

Then went round the spicy wassail bowl, drowning
every former grudge and animosity; an example worthy of modern imitation. " Wassail ! " was the word.
" Wassail ! " every guest returned as he took the circling
goblet from his friend.

In Devonshire, the Yule-log takes the form of the
Ashton fagot ; the Scandinavian tradition, that man
was created out of an ash-tree, may have originated
this idea. The fagot is composed of a bundle of ash
sticks, bound or hooped round with bands of the same
tree ; and the number of these last ought, it is said,
to be nine. It is an acknowledged and time-honored
custom, that for every *crack* which the bands of the
Ashton fagot make in bursting, when charred through,

the master of the house is bound to furnish a fresh bowl of wassail.

The Yule-log was burned until Twelfth Night. On the last day of its being in use, which in some places was even as late as Candlemas Day (February 2), a small piece of the Christmas block having been kept on purpose, the practice was, to

> "Kindle the Christmas brand, and then
> Till sunset let it burne,
> Which quenched, then lay it up agen,
> Till Christmas next returne.

> "Part must be kept, wherewith to teend
> The Christmas log next yeare;
> And where it is safely kept, the fiend
> Can do no mischief there."

There are many curious superstitions connected with the burning of the Yule-log. It is said the maidens that blow a Christmas fire should be like suitors in a law court, and come to the task with clean hands: —

> "Wash your hands, or else the fire
> Will not teend to your desire;
> Unwashed hands, ye maidens know,
> Dead the fire though ye blow."

Moreover no person that squints should be permitted to enter the room when it is lit on Christmas Eve; nor should any one barefooted be allowed to pass through the hall. In France the Yule-log was once believed to keep away pestilence from all who were seated around it, this protection extending throughout the year.

As an accompaniment to the Yule-log, a candle of enormous size, called the Yule candle, or sometimes the Wassail candle, shed its light on the festive board.

Brand, in his "Popular Antiquities," states that "in the buttery of St. John's College, Oxford, an ancient candle socket of stone still remains, ornamented with the figure of the Holy Lamb. It was formerly used for holding the Christmas candle, which, during the twelve nights of the Christmas festival, was burned on the high table at supper."

As the hall was the place where the Christmas festivities were held, — the scene of hospitality, the stronghold of old English manners and customs, — we here digress from the main object of this work to give a few interesting facts illustrative of its history, which it is hoped will enable the reader the better to picture to himself the Christmas holidays of the olden time. They are taken from Mr. Wright's "Domestic Manners and Sentiments of the Middle Ages":—

The most important part of the Saxon house was the hall. The Saxon dwelling appears to have been of wood, of which material houses continued very generally to be built, until comparatively modern times. A great change, however, was wrought in England by the entrance of the Normans. Some time after that period, or about the middle of the twelfth century, we begin to become better acquainted with the domestic manners of our forefathers, and from this time to the end of the fourteenth century the change was very gradual, and in many respects the manners and customs remained nearly the same. The " hall," or, according to the Norman word, the " salle," was still the principal part of the building; but its old Saxon character seems to have been so universally acknowledged that the first or Saxon name prevailed over the other. The name at this time usually given to the whole dwelling-house, was the Norman word " manoir," or manor; and we find this applied popularly to the houses of all classes, excepting only the cottages of laboring people.

In houses of the twelfth century, the hall, situated on the ground floor, and open to the roof, continued to form the principal feature of the building. A chamber generally adjoined one end, and at the other was usually a stable. The whole building stood within a small inclosure, consisting, in front, of a yard or court, called in Norman " aire " (area); and in the rear, of a garden which was surrounded with a hedge and ditch. In front, the house had generally one door, which was the main entrance into the hall, from which apartment there was a door into the chamber at one end; and one into the " croiche," or stable, at the other end, and a back door into the garden. The stable, as a matter of course, would have a large door, or outlet into the yard. The chief windows were those of the hall.

Alexander Neckam, Abbot of Cirencester, who died in 1217, has left us a sufficiently clear description of the Norman hall. He says that it had a vestibule or screen (vestibulum), and was entered through a porch (porticus), and that it had a court (atrium). In the interior of the hall, there were posts (or columns) placed at regular distances. The few examples of Norman halls which remain, are thus divided internally by two rows of these columns. He enumerates the materials required in the construction of the hall, which shows that he is speaking of a timber building. A fine example of one of these timber halls, though of a later period, is, or was recently, standing in the city of Gloucester, with its internal posts as here described. There appears, also, to have been an inner court-yard, in which Neckam intimates that poultry were kept. The whole building and the two court-yards were surrounded by a wall, outside of which were the garden and orchard.

At the close of the fourteenth century, the middle classes of England had made great advances in wealth and independence. This increase of wealth appears in the multiplication of articles of furniture and household implements, especially those of a more valuable description. There was also a great increase both in the number and magnitude of the houses which intervened between the castle and the cottage. Instead of having one or two bedrooms only, and turning people at night into the hall to sleep, as in earlier times, we now find whole suites of chambers; while, where before, the family lived chiefly in the hall, privacy was now sought by the addition of parlors, of which there were often more than one, in a house of ordinary size. The hall was, in fact, already beginning to diminish in relative importance to the rest of the mansion. Whether in town or country, houses of any magnitude were now generally built round an interior court, into which the rooms almost invariably looked, only small and unimportant windows looking toward the street or country. This arrangement, of course, originated in the necessity of studying security, a necessity which was never felt in England more severely than during the fifteenth century.

The hall was still but scantily furnished. The permanent furniture consisted chiefly of benches and of a seat with a back to it, for the superior members of the family. The head table, at least, which stood on a dais, or raised platform, at the upper end of the hall, was often a permanent one; and there were in general other permanent tables, or "tables dormants;" but still the majority of the tables in the hall were made up for each meal, by placing boards upon trestles. Cushions with ornamental cloths called "bankers" and "dorsers," for placing over the benches and backs of the seats of the better persons at the table, were also in general use. On special occasions, tapestry was suspended on the walls of the hall. Another article of furniture also had now become common, the "buffet," or stand on which the plate and other vessels were arranged.

A vocabulary of the fifteenth century enumerates as the ordinary furniture of the hall : "A board, a trestle, a banker, a dorser, a natte (table-cloth), a table dormant, a basin, a laver, fire on a hearth, a brand or torch, a Yule block, an andiron, tongs, a pair of bellows, wood for the fire, a long settle, a chair, a bench, a stool, a cushion, and a screen."

There were also "waits," or trumpeters, in olden time always attached to the halls of great people, to announce the commencement of the dinner. Only persons of a certain rank were allowed this piece of ostentation; but everybody who could obtain it had minstrelsy at dinner. The wandering minstrel was welcome in every hall; and for this very reason the class of ambulatory musicians was very numerous.

In the sixteenth century the hall still continued to hold its position as the great public apartment of the house, and in its arrangements it differed slightly from those of an earlier date; it was, indeed, now, the only part of the house which had not been affected by the increasing taste for domestic privacy. We have many examples of the old Gothic hall of this period in England, not only as it existed and was used in the sixteenth century, but in some cases, especially in colleges, still used for its original purposes. One of the simplest, and at the same time best examples of these halls, is found in the Hospital of St. Cross near Winchester : —

"The principal entrance to the main building from the first or outer court, opened into a *thorough lobby*, having on one side several doors or arches leading to the buttery, kitchen, and domestic offices ; on the other side, the hall, parted off by a screen, generally of wood elaborately carved, and enriched with shields and a variety of ornament, and pierced with several arches having folding doors. Above the screen and over the lobby, was the ministrels' gallery, and on its front were usually hung armor, antlers, and similar memorials of the family exploits. The hall itself was a large and lofty room, in the shape of a parallelogram ; the roof, the timbers of which were framed with pendents, richly carved and emblazoned with heraldic insignia, formed one of its most striking features. 'The top-beam of the hall ' — in allusion to the position of his coat of arms — was a symbolical manner of drinking the health of the master of the house. At the upper end of this chamber — furthest from the entrance — the floor was usually raised a step, and this part was styled the 'dais', or 'high place.' On one side of the dais was a deep embayed window, reaching nearly down to the floor ; the other windows ranged along one or both sides of the hall, at a considerable height above the ground, so as to leave room for wainscoting or arras below them. They were enriched with stained glass, representing the armorial bearings of the family, their connections, and royal patrons, and between the windows were hung full length portraits of the same persons. The royal arms, also, usually occupied a conspicuous station at either end of the room. The head table was laid for the lord and principal guests on the raised place, parallel with the upper end wall, and other tables were ranged along the sides for inferior visitors and retainers. Tables so placed were said to stand 'banquet-wise.' In the centre of the hall was the rere-dosse, or fire-iron, against which fagots were piled, and burnt upon the stone floor ; the smoke passing through an aperture in the roof immediately overhead, which was generally formed into an elevated lantern, a conspicuous ornament to the exterior of the building. In latter times a wide arched fire-place was formed in the wall on one side of the room."

The earlier half of the sixteenth century was the

period when the pageantry of feasting in these halls was carried to its greatest degree of splendor, especially at Christmas. " In the houses of the noble and wealthy, the dinner itself was laid out with great pomp, was almost always accompanied with music, and not unfrequently interrupted with dances, mummings, and masquerades."

Aubrey says: In days of yore " the lords (then lords in deed as well as title) lived in their countries like petty kings,[1] had *jura regalia* belonging to their seigniories, had their castle and boroughs, and sent burgesses to the Lower House; had gallows within their Libertie, where they could try, condemn, draw, and hang; never went to London but in Parliament-time, or once a year, to do their homage and duty to the king. The Lords of manours kept good houses in their countries, did eat in their great Gothick halls at the high table. . . . The hearth was commonly in the middle, as at most colleges, whence the saying ' Round about our coal-fire.' Here in the halls were the mummings, cob-loaf stealing, and great number of old Christmas plays performed." The halls of all the colleges, at the Universities of Oxford and Cambridge, and in the Inns of Court, still remain as in Aubrey's time, accurate examples of the ancient baronial and conventual halls; preserving not merely their original

---

[1] " Heretofore noblemen and gentlemen of fair estates had their heralds, who wore their coat-of-arms at Christmas, and at other solemn times, and cried ' Largesse ' thrice."

form and appearance, but the identical arrangement and service of the tables.

The following imaginary scene from the London " Holiday Book," gives us a very good idea of the appearance of one of these old English halls on a Christmas Eve : —

" A fire on the wide hearth-stone ; an oaken table ; with a goodly company ; closed doors ; the mistletoe aloft upon a mighty beam ; evergreens abundant ; the '*Minstrels*' in the tapestried gallery ; quaint figures of '*Mummers*' drolly attired, peep from behind the half-drawn curtains, dependent before the recess of the deep bay-windows."

From time to time it appears that the gentry and nobility of the realm were admonished by royal authority of their duty to go down to their country seats, and then and there to entertain their friends and neighbors with liberal hospitality.

It is said that at Houghton Chapel, Nottingham-shire, "*the good Sir William Hollis*," who kept his house in great splendor and hospitality, began Christmas at All Hallow-tide (October 31), and continued it till Candlemas (February 2); during which time *any man* was permitted to stay three days, without being asked who he was, or whence he came.

In the " Diary " of the Rev. John Ward, Vicar of Stratford-upon-Avon, extending from 1648 to 1679, it is stated that the Duke of Norfolk expended £20,000 in keeping Christmas. Charles II. gave over keeping this festival for economy's sake, having so many other expenses he could not very well afford to keep Christ-mas.

From this time "keeping hall" at Christmas is said to have declined.

The following programme of Christmas hospitalities to be observed in a baronial hall will appropriately con-clude the subject : —

"On Christmas-day, service in the church ended, the gentlemen presently repair into the hall to breakfast, with brawn, mustard, and malmsey.

"At dinner, the butler, appointed for the Christmas, is to see the tables covered and furnished : and the ordinary butlers of the house are decently to set bread, napkins, and trenchers, in good form, at every table ; with spoones and knives. At the first course, is served a fair and large boar's head, upon a silver platter, with min-stralsye.

"Two 'servants' are to attend at supper, and to bear two fair torches of wax, next before the musicians and trumpeters, and stand above the fire with the musick, till the first course be served in through the hall. Which performed, they, with the musick, are to return into the buttery. The like course is to be observed in all things, during the time of Christmas.

"At night, before supper, are revels and dancing, and so also after supper, during the twelve daies of Christmas. The Master of the Revels is, after dinner and supper, to sing a caroll, or song; and command other gentlemen then there present to sing with him and the company ; and so it is very decently performed." [1]

[1] Nichol's *Progresses and Processions of Queen Elizabeth*, vol. i., pp. 20, 21, anno 1562.

CHAPTER V.

CHRIST-
MAS
Was-
sail
has been from the
earliest time associated
with our notions of
Christmas in the Hall.
This famous beverage
was served smoking hot,
and might be made of
wine, cider, or ale, which
besides being sweetened
and spiced, was also
" *augmented* " by the addition of a toast and
apples stuck full of
cloves.[1] When ale was
used the compound was
called Lamb's Wool.

[1] The " Mark Lane Express " gives the following receipt for making the wassail-bowl : Simmer a small quantity of the following spices in a teacupful of

Herrick says : —

> "Next crown the bowl full
> With gentle lamb's wool :
> Add sugar, nutmeg, and ginger,
> With store of ale too ;
> And thus must ye do,
> To make the wassail a swinger ! "

According to the author of " Nooks and Corners of English Life," this term Lamb's Wool was derived from the Irish words " *La Mas Ubal*," signifying the Feast or Day of the Apple, and pronounced " *Lamasool*," which term soon passed into " *Lamb's Wool.*"

In some of the Southern States a similar beverage, under the name of " Apple Jack " is still a customary drink at Christmas, rum and water being substituted for ale.

According to an ancient tradition, mentioned by Geoffrey of Monmouth and other monkish writers, the origin of this custom of Wassailing is traced to Rowena, the daughter of the Saxon Hengist. Richard Verstegan (1605) says : —

water ; namely, Cardamums, cloves, nutmeg, mace, ginger, cinnamon, and coriander. When done, put the spice to two, four, or six bottles of port, sherry, or madeira, with one pound and a half of fine loaf sugar (pounded) to four bottles, and set all on the fire in a clean, bright saucepan ; meanwhile, have yolks of twelve and the whites of six eggs well whisked up in it. Then, when the spiced and sugared wine is a little warm, take out one teacupful ; and so on for three or four cups ; after which, when it boils, add the whole of the remainder, pouring it in gradually, and stirring it briskly all the time, so as to froth it. The moment a fine froth is obtained, toss in twelve fine soft roasted apples, and send it up hot. Spices for each bottle of wine : 10 grains of mace, 46 grains of cloves, 37 grains of cardamums, 28 grains of cinnamon, 12 grains of nutmeg, 48 grains of ginger, 49 grains of coriander seeds."

"As this lady was very beautiful, so was she of a very comely deportment; and Hingistus, having invited King Vortiger to a supper at his new builded castle, caused that after supper she came forth of her chamber into the king's presence, with a cup of gold filled with wine in her hand, and making in very seemly manner a low reverence unto the king, said with a pleasing grace and countenance, 'Waes-heal, hlaford Cyning' — 'Be of health, Lord King.'

"Of the beauty of this lady the king took so great liking, that he became exceedingly inamored with her, and desired to have her in marriage, which Hingistus agreed unto, upon condition that the king should give unto him the whole country of Kent, whereunto he willingly condescended and divorcing himself from his former married wife, married with the Saxon Lady Rowena."

An early authority, Robert of Gloucester, thus commemorates the event : —

"𝕽𝖚𝖘𝖙𝖊 𝖍𝖎𝖗𝖊 𝖆𝖓𝖉 𝖘𝖎𝖙𝖙𝖊 𝖍𝖎𝖗𝖊 𝖆𝖉𝖔𝖚𝖓𝖊 𝖆𝖓𝖉 𝖌𝖑𝖆𝖉 𝖉𝖗𝖔𝖓𝖐𝖊 𝖍𝖎𝖗𝖊 𝖍𝖊𝖎𝖑

𝕬𝖓𝖉 𝖙𝖍𝖆𝖙 𝖜𝖆𝖘 𝖙𝖍𝖔 𝖎𝖓 𝖙𝖍𝖎𝖘 𝖑𝖆𝖓𝖉 𝖙𝖍𝖊 𝖇𝖊𝖗𝖘𝖙 𝖜𝖆𝖘=𝖍𝖆𝖎𝖑

𝕬𝖘. 𝖎𝖓 𝕷𝖆𝖓𝖌𝖚𝖆𝖌𝖊 𝖔𝖋 𝕾𝖆𝖗𝖔𝖅𝖓𝖊 𝖙𝖍𝖆𝖙 𝖜𝖊 𝖒𝖎𝖌𝖍𝖙 𝖊𝖇𝖊𝖗𝖊 𝖎𝖜𝖎𝖙𝖊

𝕬𝖓𝖉 𝖘𝖔 𝖜𝖊𝖑𝖑 𝖍𝖊 𝖕𝖆𝖎𝖙𝖍 𝖙𝖍𝖊 𝖋𝖔𝖑𝖊 𝖆𝖇𝖔𝖚𝖙. 𝖙𝖍𝖆𝖙 𝖍𝖊 𝖎𝖘 𝖓𝖔𝖙 𝖅𝖚𝖙 𝖇𝖔𝖗𝖌𝖚𝖙𝖊."

Or, according to a more modern version: —

"'Health, my lord king,' the sweet Rowena said ;
'Health,' cry'd the chieftain, to the Saxon maid ;
Then gayly 'rose, and 'midst the concourse wide,
Kiss'd her hale lips, and placed her by his side ;
At the soft scene such gentle thoughts abound,
That health and kisses 'mongst the guests went round ;
From this the social custom took its rise,
We still retain, and must forever prize."

The mistletoe or kissing-bush appears to have been early associated with Christmas wassailing. Since the

days of Queen Elizabeth, the custom has been to sus-
pend a bunch of the mistletoe from the wall or ceiling
on Christmas Eve. Any one of the fair sex who by
chance, or possibly *on purpose*, passes beneath the mystic branch is summarily kissed by any of the male sex
who chooses to avail himself of the privilege. At the
same time he should wish her a happy New Year and
present her with one of the berries for good luck's
sake. But with the disappearance of the berries the
sport should come to an end.

The origin of the rites and ceremonies practiced beneath the mistletoe seems to be clouded by the haze of
uncertainty not unlike that which surrounds the origin
of the Eleusinian Mysteries.

The plant was looked upon by our Pagan ancestors
with a species of veneration. It is supposed to have
been the sacred branch referred to by Virgil in his description of the descent to the lower regions; and, if
so, may be presumed to have been in use in the religious ceremonies of the Greeks and Romans, as this
description is considered an allegorical representation
of some of their mysteries. It is well known that the
mistletoe was held sacred by the Druids and the Celtic
nations. The Gothic nations also attached extraordinary qualities to it, and it is said in the Edda to have
been the cause of the death of Balder — the god of
poetry and eloquence.

At Jul or Yule, — the feast of the winter solstice, —
the Druids used to gather the mistletoe with mys-

terious ceremony. It was cut from the oak with a golden sickle by the chief of the Druids himself, clothed in white : white bulls and even human sacrifices are said to have been offered. These sacrifices were followed by a variety of festivities.

When gathered, the mistletoe was "divided into small portions and distributed among the people, who hung up the sprays over the entrance to their dwellings as a propitiation and shelter to the sylvan deities during the season of frost and cold."

Only those oaks which had the mistletoe upon them were held sacred by the Druids. " The reverence of the people towards the priests," says Mr. Hervey, " as well as their estimation of the mistletoe, proceeded in great measure from the cures which the former effected by means of the plant. Medicinal properties, we believe, are still ascribed to it, and it was not long since deemed efficacious in the subduing of convulsive disorders. Sir John Colback, in his dissertation concerning it, observes that this beautiful plant must have been designed by the Almighty 'for further and more noble purposes than barely to feed thrushes, or to be hung up surreptitiously in houses to drive away evil spirits.' Against the latter, it appears to have been used as a charm, up to the last century." Coles, in the " Art of Simpling " (1656), says, that " If any one hang mistletoe about the neck the witches can have no power of him."

Ecclesiastical councils have, from time to time, for-

bidden the use of the mistletoe. Other Pagan ceremonies have been tolerated, or by adaptation, hallowed
to Christian uses. Not so with the mistletoe, which
in spite of its innocent-looking berries, has never been
allowed to share in "benefit of clergy." Indeed, the
priests and monks of the Middle Ages regarded the
plant with superstitious horror, being in their celibate
state unable to comprehend its attractive influence, except on the supposition of diabolical agency.

According to a writer in "Notes and Queries," "mistletoe formerly had a place amongst Christmas decorations for churches, but was afterwards excluded. In
the earlier ages of the Church, many festivities not
tending to edification had crept in, mutual kissing
amongst the number; but as this soon led to inde-
corum, kissing and mistletoe were both very properly
bundled out of the Church."

According to Archdeacon Nares, the tradition is
"that the maid who was not kissed under it at Christmas would not be married that year."

In some places people try lots by the crackling of
the leaves and berries in the fire.

The mistletoe has become in modern times an article
of commerce. From the statistics of this peculiar
branch of trade, it would seem that Herefordshire
produces the largest supply of any one county in England. As many as one hundred and twelve or one
hundred and fourteen tons have been sent out of this
western county in one season, besides many tons for-

warded to foreign countries, and the trade is said to be annually increasing.

But if kissing at Christmas was regulated by the use of the mistletoe, wassailing appears to have been restricted by no such statute of limitation, for long after the berries of the mistletoe had disappeared, " the jolly wassail bowl went round."

The custom seems to have been observed in the monasteries as well as in private houses. In front of the abbot, at the upper end of the refectory table, was placed the mighty bowl, styled in their language, *Po̩- culum Caritatis*, and from it the Superior drank to all, and all drank in succession to each other.

The Lord Arundel of Wardour has now in his possession a fine specimen of a wassail bowl of undoubted Anglo-saxon work, formerly belonging to the Abbey of Glastonbury; it holds two quarts, and originally had eight pegs inside, dividing the liquor into half-pints; on the lid is carved the Crucifixion, with the Virgin and St. John, one on each side; and round the cup are carved the Twelve Apostles.

A relic of the ancient custom of wassailing still exists in the usage of certain corporation festivals. The person presiding stands up at the close of dinner, and drinks from a flagon, usually of silver, having a handle on each side, by which he holds it with each hand, and the toast-master announces him as drinking " the health of his brethren out of the ' *loving cup*.'" The *loving cup*, which is the ancient *wassail bowl* is then passed to the guest on his left hand, and by him to *his* left hand neighbor, and as it finds its way round the room to each guest in his turn, so each stands up and drinks to the president.

Bishop Cox, in his " Impressions of England," describing one of these festivals, — a dinner given by the Lord Mayor of London to the S. P. G., in 1851, — says, " The toast-master appeared behind his Lordship's chair and began : ' My Lord Archbishop of Canterbury, my Lord Bishop of London,' and so on through the roll of bishops — ' my lords, ladies, and gentlemen, the Lord Mayor and Lady Mayoress greet you in a loving cup and give you a hearty welcome.'

" The Mayor and Mayoress then rose, and taking the loving cup in hand, she uncovered it for him, with a graceful courtesy, to which he returned a bow, and then drank, wiped the chalice with his napkin, allowed it to be covered, and then sat down, while the lady, turning to the Archbishop, who rose accordingly, repeated the ceremony, save that he uncovered the cup, and it was her turn to taste the draught. Thus the cup went round."

CHAPTER VI.

CHRISTMAS MUMMERIES.

HE custom of representing at every solemn festival of the Church some event recorded in Scripture, became general in Christendom at a very early period. Gregory Nazianzen, Patriarch of Constantinople, and others eminent in the Church, dramatized portions of the Old and New Testament, and substituted them for the Greek plays still publicly represented in their day. They were modeled on those of the ancient Greek tragedy, the choruses being turned into Christian hymns. One only of Gregory Nazianzen's plays — a tragedy called "Christ's Passion" — is extant. "The Christians found, in the wit and elegance of his writings, all that they could desire in the heathen poets."

Following the example of the Fathers, the clergy of the Middle Ages devised the mystery and miracle plays, with the view of interesting and instructing the people, a method which the parables of our Lord might be said to justify. The Bible and Church service being then in an unknown tongue, it may readily be believed that the simple folk of those days derived the greater part of their theological and biblical knowledge from such religious shows. The mystery and miracle plays were composed of scriptural incidents, or, as Fitz-Stephen informs us, of "Representations of those miracles that were wrought by holy confessors; or those passions and sufferings in which the martyrs so signally displayed their fortitude. The actors were the scholars of the clergy; the church itself was frequently used as the place of exhibition; and the rich vestments and sacred furniture employed in the church service were sometimes permitted to be used by the performers, to give superior truth and lustre to their representations."

Thus, on some special saint's day, says Mr. Wright, the choral boys, or the younger clergy, would perform "some striking act in the life of the saint commemorated, or, on particular festivals of the Church, those

incidents of gospel history to which the festival especially related. By degrees, a rather more imposing
character was given to these performances by the addition of a continuous dialogue, which, however, was
written in Latin verse, and was no doubt chanted.
This incipient drama, in Latin, as far as we know it,
belongs to the twelfth century, and is represented by
a large number of examples still preserved in mediæval
manuscripts. Some of the earliest of these have for
their author a pupil of the celebrated Abelard, who
lived in the first half of the twelfth century, named
Hilarius, and is understood to have been by birth an
Englishman. Hilarius appears as a playful Latin poet,
and among a number of short pieces, which may be
almost called lyric; he has left us three of these religious plays. The subject of the first is the raising of
Lazarus from the Dead, the chief peculiarity of which
consists of the songs of Lamentation, placed in the
mouths of the two sisters of Lazarus, Mary and Mar-
tha. The second represents one of the miracles attributed to St. Nicholas; and the third, the history of
Daniel. The latter is longer and more elaborate than
the others, and at its conclusion, the stage directions
tell us that, "if it were performed at matins, Darius,
king of the Medes and Persians, was to chant *Te Deum
Laudamus;* but if it were at vespers, the great king
was to chant *Magnificat Anima mea Dominum.*"

"These church plays," continues Mr. Wright, "consisted of two descriptions of subjects: they either rep-

resented the miraculous acts of certain saints, which had a plain meaning; or some incident taken from Holy Scripture, which was supposed to have a hidden, mysterious signification, as well as an apparent one; and hence the one class of subjects was usually spoken of simply as *miraculum*, a miracle; and the other as *mysterium*, a mystery."

At a later day appeared the moralities, or allegorical dramas.

To relieve the gravity of these performances, and to add to their popularity, interludes, or farcical representations were introduced. These became so exceedingly popular with the masses, that the religious character of the play or drama was soon lost sight of in the buffoonery that accompanied them.

" We have a proof," says Mr. Wright, " that the Latin religious plays, and the festivities in which they were employed, had become greatly developed in the twelfth century, in the notice taken of them in the ecclesiastical councils of that period. So early as the papacy of Gregory VIII., the pope urged the clergy 'to extirpate' from their churches these theatrical plays, and other festive practices, which were not quite in harmony with the sacred character of the buildings." Similar prohibition of the acting of such plays in churches are met with at subsequent periods.

 In spite of ecclesiastical censures, however, they continued to flourish, being taken up by the guilds and municipal corporations. Certain annual religious festivals were still the occasions on which the plays were acted; but they were taken entirely out of the churches, and the performances took place in the open streets. Each guild in a town had its pageant, and its own actors, who performed in masks and costumes, and each had one of a series of plays, which were performed at places where they halted in the procession.

In the reign of Richard II., dramas were represented by the society of parish clerks. The fraternity had been incorporated into a guild about the year 1240, under the patronage of St. Nicholas. Chaucer has painted the parish clerk as the jolly Absolon, in a white surplice, with curly hair, red stockings, and fashionable shoes. " It was anciently customary," says Mr. Godwin, "for men and women of the first quality, ecclesiastics and others, who were lovers of church music, to be admitted into this corporation; and they gave large gratuities for the support and education of persons practiced in this art. This society were usually hired as a band of vocal performers to assist at the funerals of the nobility or other distinguished persons.

In the year 1391, the society played interludes in the fields at Skinner's Well for three days, Richard the Second, with his queen and court, being among the spectators. Again, in the year 1409, the clerks played at Skinner's Well, for eight days, " Matter from the Creation of the World," a great assembly of the noblemen of England being present. The " Matter from the Creation of the World," meant, doubtless, such a

cycle of Scripture histories, from the creation down-
wards, as is to be found in the extant sets of Miracle
Plays, performed at York, Chester, and Coventry.

In the sixteenth century the Reformers, so far from
condemning these entertainments, themselves, com-
piled plays, not only for the purpose of exposing the
corruptions of the Church, but with the view also of
instructing the people in faith and morals. Many of
these plays are still extant. Bishop Bale, the author of
" God's Promises ; a Tragedy or Interlude," does not
scruple to put upon the theatrical stage, an imperson-
ation of the heavenly Father. A still more remarkable piece of irreverence is to be found in his play,
entitled, " Brefe Comedy, or Enterlude of Johan Bap-
tystes preachyng in the Wyldernesse," etc. The actors
in this piece are Pater Cœlestis, Joannes Baptistes,
Publicanus, Pharisæus, Jesus Christus, Turba Vulga-
ris, Miles Armatus, and Sadducæus.

Among the devices employed in its representation
was a mechanical contrivance which produced a sem-
blance of the Holy Ghost descending in the form of
a dove, "*Descendit tunc*," runs one of the stage directions, "*super Christum Spiritus Sanctus in columbæ
specie, et vox patris de cœlo audietur hoc modo.*" Moreover, in his play of "Kyng Johan," Bale has not hesi-
tated to introduce indecent jests, the coarseness of
which rivaled those of a much earlier age. " This
play," an edition of which was recently published by
the Camden Society, " is not only a remarkable work

of a remarkable man," says Mr. Wright, "but it may be considered as the first rude model of the English historical drama." [1]

The "*ludi*," or CHRISTMAS plays, formerly exhibited at court, were of quite a different character from those described above. It is said they can be traced back certainly as far as the reign of Edward III.; and they are by some thought to be much older. The dresses appropriated in 1348 to one of these plays, show that they were mummeries, and not theatrical divertisements. The King (Edward III.) then kept his Christmas at his Castle at Guildford, the "keep" of which remains to this day. The dresses on that occasion, it is said, consisted of eighty tunics of buckram of various colors; forty-two vizors; fourteen faces of women; fourteen of men; and fourteen heads of angels made with silver; twenty-eight crests; fourteen mantles embroidered with heads of dragons; fourteen white tunics, wrought with the heads and wings of peacocks; fourteen with the heads and wings of swans; fourteen tunics, painted with the eyes of peacocks; fourteen tunics of English linen, painted; and fourteen other tunics embroidered with stars of gold.

The magnificent pageants and disguisings frequently exhibited at court, in succeeding reigns, and especially in the reign of Henry VIII., were but a species of

[1] "Many years after our drama was mature," says Mr. Morley, "reminders of its old ways lingered at Bartholomew Fair, and there, perhaps, took place the last performance of a miracle play in this country."

mummeries destitute of character and humor; their chief aim being to surprise the spectators "by the ridiculous and exaggerated oddity of the vizors, and by the singularity and splendor of the dresses; — everything was out of nature and propriety."

Stowe thus describes a remarkable mummery made by the citizens of London in 1377, for the disport of the young Prince Richard, son to the Black Prince:—

"They rode, disguised and well horsed, 130 in number, with minstrels and torch-lights of wax, to Kennington beside Lambeth, where the young.Prince remained with his mother. These maskers alighted, entered the Palace Hall, and set to the Prince and his mother and lords, cups and rings of gold, which they won at a cast; after which they feasted, and the Prince and lords danced with the mummers, which jollity being ended, they were made to drink," etc.

The plays exhibited in the country at this season appear to have been of a more mixed character. Such were the Cornish mummeries, or miracle plays; which were never performed as elsewhere in churches, but in an earthen amphitheatre in some open field. These continued to be exhibited long after the abolition of the miracle plays and moralities in other parts of the kingdom. Accordingly we find them lingering in Cornwall even to the present time; and there, as also in Devonshire and Staffordshire, the old spirit of Christmas is kept up with great earnestness.

In the North of England there remains a species of mumming called the sword dance. "This," says

Mr. Henderson, "may yet be looked for in most towns from the Humber to the Cheviot Hills." There are some trifling local variations both in dance and song; the latter has altered with the times; the former is plainly a relic of the war dances of our Danish and Saxon ancestors. Tacitus thus describes a sword dance among the ancient Germans : —

"One public diversion was constantly exhibited at all their meetings; young men, who by frequent exercise have attained to great perfection in that pastime, strip themselves, and dance among the points of swords and spears, with most wonderful agility, and even with the most elegant and graceful motions. They do not perform this dance for hire, but for the entertainment of the spectators, esteeming their applause a sufficient reward."

Mr. Brand also tells us that he has seen this dance frequently performed in the North of England, about Christmas, with little or no variation from the ancient method; and Washington Irving refers to the custom in the "Sketch Book."

There is also a relic of the ancient mystery and miracle plays to be found in the more modern Christmas mummeries; especially in that popular play of "St. George and the Dragon." This is still represented in some parts of England by a sort of dramatic corps headed by "Father Christmas." [1] These mummers go abroad and about the country on Christmas Eve, performing this mock play in the halls of the gentry and in the kitchens of farm-houses.

[1] See Appendix.

According to the "Golden Legend," on which this
old play is founded, the city of Sylene, being infested
with a dragon in the marsh, and the sheep failing, —
which had been given, two a day, to prevent his hurt-
ing the people, — an ordinance substituted children
and young people, to be chosen by lot, whether rich
or poor. The king's daughter was drawn, and St.
George happening to pass by when she was on her
way to be devoured, fought and killed the dragon.

This legend is doubtless based on the spiritual combat mentioned in the Apocalypse, in which Michael
the Archangel triumphs over "that old serpent, the
Devil."

In 1849 this still very popular drama of "St. George
and the Dragon" was acted on the floor of the Free
Trade Hall in Manchester, where it is customary
to celebrate the Epiphany, called Old Christmas or
Twelfth Day, with many ancient forms and ceremonies.

Before closing this subject a few words should be
said in regard to the Christmas tree, a representation
of which forms the initial letter of this chapter.

This most picturesque of mediæval pageants, tow-
ering aloft with undiminished glory, festooned with
garlands of gold and silver paper, sparkling with its
myriad lights, still presents an enchanting vision to
thousands of happy children here as well as abroad.

The custom of decorating the Christmas tree is of
great antiquity, and is even supposed to be of Pagan

origin. "The Christian Remembrancer" (1868), speaking of it, says that Chevalier Bunsen contributed to Christianize a heathen custom "by placing a picture of the Madonna della Seggiola amid the tapers so as to illuminate the loveliest infant representation of Him who brought good gifts unto men ; and thus to sanctify the ancient German custom of hanging gifts on a tree, dating from the time of heathen life in a forest."

However, the representation of the Christ-child appears to have figured in the decorations of the tree from a very early date.

In Scandinavian countries the custom is to dress up some one — usually a young girl — as the Christ-child, with a crown of gilt-foil, and fair outstretched wings of white paper.

It is said, that Luther, in his family, celebrated Christmas Eve according to the German custom. In an engraving, published in Leipsic, the great Reformer, who was fond of children and music, is thus represented playing upon a gittern, an instrument not unlike the modern guitar.

The Christmas tree has been but recently introduced into England and America, although in Pennsylvania, where many of the settlers are of German origin, there has been an observance of the custom from early Colony times. Christmas Eve is there observed with many of the ceremonies practiced in the Fatherland. The Christmas tree branches forth in all its splendor, and the Christ-child, according to the German legend, comes flying through the air on golden wings, and causes the bough to produce in the night all manner of fruit, gilt sweetmeats, apples, nuts, etc., for the good children.

In Germany, accompanying the Christmas tree, there is a personification of the good St. Nicholas, known as Pumpernickel or Pelsnickol, that is, Nicholas with the Fur. He is usually represented with a long gray beard, a hooded cloak spotted with snow-flakes, a bundle over his shoulder, a toy in one hand, and a bundle of rods in the other; or else he appears in a long furred pelisse, trimmed with ivy-leaves, with a green sash round his waist, and a bear-skin cap on his head.

There is usually, especially in the Rhineland,[1] a carpet of moss surrounding the tree, with a little landscape, often very beautiful and expensive, made of toy-houses, sheep, cattle, and men, adorned with running water, and everything to make it look as natural as possible. This landscape is an important part of the Christmas tree, and is called the *Krippe* or manger.

In Roman Catholic countries there is also a scenic representation of the Nativity. There is the manger with the holy babe, the Blessed Virgin and St. Joseph, the magi, the shepherds and their flocks; but instead of being arranged around the Christmas tree, as in Protestant Germany, they are exhibited in the side-

---

[1] "In the Rhineland one can buy for a few *groschen*, in the toy-shops, large cardboard *Krippes*, which are intended to be cut out, gummed together, and placed under the Christmas trees." — *Hartford Churchman*, Jan. 1, 1876.

aisle or chapel of a church. John Locke, the philosopher, in a letter dated from Cleves in 1664, says: "Near the high altar, in the principal church at Cleves, was a little altar for the service of Christmas Day. The scene was a stable, wherein was an ox, an ass, a cradle, the Virgin, the Babe, Joseph, shepherds and angels, *dramatis personæ*. Had they but given them motion, it had been a perfect puppet-play, and might have deserved pence a-piece; for they were of the same size and make that our English puppets are; and, I am confident, these shepherds and this Joseph are kin to that Judith and Holofernes which I had seen at Bartholomew Fair."

At the Franciscan Church, in Rome, these representations are famous and costly, and still attract throngs of admiring worshipers. Goethe, writing from Rome in 1787, describes such a dramatic Christmas-Eve service in one of the churches: "The music was so arranged, that in its tone nothing belonging to pastoral music was wanting, — neither the singing of the shepherds, nor the twittering of birds, nor the bleating of sheep."

The following anecdote, from a French writer, proves that mediæval dramatic representations or religious shows had not quite fallen into disuse even in the beginning of this nineteenth century: "In 1821, a priest was appointed, shortly before Christmas, the curate of a village in Flanders, of whose customs he was ignorant. He had just begun the Midnight Mass,

5

when he was startled by seeing an artificial star flashing above his head. At this signal the doors of the Church opened and forthwith there entered several shepherds and shepherdesses, leaping and dancing with joy and leading some of their sheep. The curate, bewildered with the scene, wished to interpose his authority; he was as little understood by the shepherds as their sheep; the latter, as well as the former, persisting in the singular ceremony till it was concluded. Offerings of eggs and of cheese were then laid at the foot of the holy cradle (or crache), and the exulting throng departed."

CHAPTER VII.

MONG the religious shows, which, like the mystery and miracle plays, gave life and animation to the Christmas festivities of our forefathers, were the ceremonies attendant upon the installation of the mock prelate known as the Boy or Barne-Bishop.

" The accounts of the origin of this curious custom have been," says Mr. Fosbrooke," *elucidated* into *obscurity*." It is said to have been founded on this story in the " Legend of St. Nicholas " : —

"A bishop who had been elected to a vacant see, was warned by a dream to go to the doors of the church at the hour of matins, and 'hym that sholde fyrste come to the chyrche, and have the name of Nicholas, they sholde sacre hym Bissop,'—that is, one bishop was superceded by another." — *Gold. Leg.* 29 b.

" The memory of this saint and Bishop Nicholas was thus solemnized by a child," says Dr. Tanner, Bishop of St. Asaph (1732), "the better to remember the holy man, even when he was a child, and his child-like vertues, when he became a man. The Popish festival tells us, that while he lade in his cradle, he fasted Wednesdays and Fridays, sucking but once a day on those days. And his meekness and simplicity, the proper vertues of children, he maintained from his childhood as long as he lived: *And therefore,* saith the Festival, *children don him worship* before all other saints."

"The ceremony of the Boy Bishop prevailed in England as early as the reign of Edward the First; for that Prince, on his way to Scotland, in the year 1299, permitted one of these boy bishops to say vespers before him in his chapel at Heton, near Newcastle-upon-Tyne, making a present to the performers of forty shillings, no inconsiderable sum in those days." — *Wardrobe Account,* 28 Ed. I.

Hone, on this subject, says : —

"Anciently, on the 6th of December (St. Nicholas' Day), the choir-boys in cathedral and collegiate churches chose one of their number to maintain the state and authority of a bishop; for which purpose he was habited in rich episcopal robes, wore a mitre on his head, and bore a crozier in his hand;[1] his fellows for the time

---

[1] See Appendix, *Northumberland Household Book.*

being assuming the character and dress of priests, yielding him canonical obedience, taking possession of the church, and, except mass, performing all the ceremonies and offices, and on Holy Innocents' Day, actually preaching a sermon to the assembled congregation."

There is a monument of such a child-bishop who died while in office, situated on the north side of Salisbury Cathedral, on which is sculptured the figure of a youth clad in episcopal robes, with his foot on a lion-headed and dragon-tailed monster, in allusion to the expression of the Psalmist, "Thou shalt tread on the lion and the dragon."

Although there resulted much actual profanity from the above prescribed ritualistic observances, yet there seems to have been nothing irreverent intended by them, for we find that whatever was strictly sacramental in its nature, or that properly belonged to the priestly office, was not originally permitted or exercised by these mimic prelates.

"Our ancestors," says Fosbrooke, "used all these mummeries, as we now do the catechism, to impress principles upon the minds of their children."

The election of this "Episcopus Puerorum," or Episcopus *Choristorum*, always took place on St. Nicholas' Day in England, and as St. Nicholas was the patron saint of school-boys and choristers, the Boy-Bishop naturally became identified in name with his patron saint. Thus, "St. Nicholas," as he was called, became a person of great consequence, perambulating both town and country, habited as a bishop, "in pontificalibus," with his fellow choristers also in appropriate vestments, singing carols, etc., being in fact Christmas personified, or "Old Father Christmas."

From a printed church-book containing the service of the Boy-Bishop, set to music, we learn that on the eve of Innocents' Day, the Boy-Bishop and his youthful clergy, in their copes, and with burning tapers in their hands, went in solemn procession, chanting and singing versicles as they walked into the choir by the west door, in such order that the dean and canons went foremost, the chaplains next, and the Boy-Bishop, with his priests, in the last and highest place. He then took his seat, and the rest of the children disposed themselves upon each side of the choir, upon the uppermost ascent; the canons *resident* (reversing the usual order) bearing the incense and the book, and the petit-canons the tapers, according to the Rubric. Afterwards he proceeded to the altar of the Holy Trinity and All Saints, which he first censed, and next the Image of the Holy Trinity, his priests all the while singing. Then they all chanted a service with prayers and responses, and, in the like manner taking his seat, the Boy-Bishop repeated salutations, prayers, and versicles; and, in conclusion, gave his benediction to the people, the chorus answering, "Deo Gratias." After he received his crozier from the cross-bearer, other ceremonies were performed, and he chanted the compline; turning toward the choir he delivered an exhortation, and last of all pronounced the benediction.

In process of time, however, all this seemingly orderly behavior was changed for the worse. It appeared that boys would be boys, and that they mixed up with these regularly appointed services the buffooneries of the so-called " Feast of Fools," and of " The Ass," and instead of psalms and hymns, were now " sung or said " indecent songs and jests; and in place of the fragrance of incense, there were substituted all sorts of unsavory abominations.

The " Festum Fatuorum," or Feast of Fools, was more ancient and more widely celebrated than the Feast of the Ass. It may be traced in all ages of the Church, and in all parts of Christendom. It was, in fact, the old heathen festival of the January Calends. Council after council attest that all regular ecclesiastical authority perpetually opposed these festivals.[1]

According to Maitland, these farcical entertainments were not exhibited in churches until comparatively

---

[1] The Council of Rome, A. D. 744, forbids celebrating New Year's Day with pagan ceremonies. The Council of Paris, 1213, enjoins the abolition of the Festival of Fools, celebrated every 1st of January. The Council of Cognac, 1260, " Forbids *an ancient custom* of dancing within the Church on the day of the Festival of the Holy Innocents, and choosing a mock bishop." The Council of Saltzburg, 1274, abolishes the sport practiced by ecclesiastics in their churches called the Boy Bishop. Council of Toledo or Arenda (Dec. 5, 1473), forbids the custom of performing at certain times spectacles, etc., and singing songs and uttering profane discourses in churches. The Council of Narbonne, 1551, forbids shows, dances, etc., in churches on festival days, and the Council of Florence forbids every sort of scenic representation by the clergy without the Bishop's written permission.

modern times.   He cites, for authority, a writer of the
twelfth century, said to have belonged to the Church of
Amiens, who mentioned that there were some churches
in which it was customary for the bishops and archbishops to join in the Christmas games, which went on
in the monasteries in their dioceses, and even so far to
relax as to play at ball; but this is the only account he
had met of any participation by the Church (during the
dark ages), in this " Libertas Decembrica," as it was
called.

Du Cange shows that something like a mock consecration of the Bishop of Fools was performed in the
East in the ninth century, by the laity in derision of
the clergy, and that it was forbidden by the Church; a
Council declaring it to be a thing before unheard of.
According to Fosbroke some lay Greeks introduced
this singular custom into the West: —

"About the year 990 the Patriarch Theophylact invented or
adopted religious pantomimes or farces, since known by the name
of Feast of Fools, Feast of the Ass, Feast of the Innocents, etc.,
in the hopes of weaning the people from the bacchanalian and cal-
endary rules and other pagan ceremonies by the substitution of
Christian spectacles. These spectacles passed into Italy. On the
day of the festival (which Cowel makes the Caput Anni, or New
Year's Day), all the petty Canons elected an Abbot of Fools, who
after the ceremony and Te Deum, was chaired to a place where the
others were assembled. At his entrance all arose, and even the
Bishop, if present, was bound to pay him homage. Wine, fruit, and
spices were next served to him. Singing, hissing, howling, shout-
ing, etc., then followed, one party against another. A short dia-

logue succeeded; after which a porter made a mock sermon. They then went out into the town, cracking jokes upon everybody whom they met. In these visits which lasted every day from the vigil of Christmas till the evening, the Abbot wore a dress, whether a mantle, tabard, or cope with a hoop of vair; it was his place, if anything indecorous was done in the choir, to correct and chastise it. On the Feast of Innocents, a Fool-Bishop was elected in the same manner as the Abbot of Fools, and chaired with a little bell rung before, to the house of the Bishop, where the gates were to be immediately thrown open, and the mock prelate placed in a principal window, where he stood and gave the benediction towards the town."

In Paris from A. D. 1198 to 1438 the Festival of Fools was held on the first of January, when all sorts of absurdities were perpetrated. It appears from an encyclical of the theologians of Paris, 1444, referred to by Du Cange, that latterly the clergy encouraged these fooleries, and attempted to purify them by mixing up with them fastings and entertainments.

The so-called " Feast of the Ass " does not appear to have been always among these mere farcical entertainments, but to have had sometimes a more serious and dignified character, at least such was that celebrated in the cathedral at Rouen. Du Cange gives from the ordinal of that cathedral, the office or rubric, or stage directions of the office appointed for the Feast of Asses, which was a sort of interlude annually performed at Rouen and in some other churches at Christmas. It is a manuscript of the fifteenth century, but it contains only the initiatory words of each part; the *dramatis personæ* appear to have been numerous and miscellaneous. From the description, it might be very properly termed a Miracle Play. There were Jews and Gentiles, the representatives of their various bodies; all the prophets of the Old Testament and the Sibyl[1] were personified, variously attired, and predicting the birth of the Redeemer. Moses being arrayed in an albe and cope, with the appearance of a horned glory over his head, a long beard and a staff, and the Tables of the Law in his hands; Amos as an old man with a beard, holding an ear of wheat; Isaiah in an albe with a red stole bound round his head, and a long beard; Jeremiah in the vestments of a priest, a long beard and a scroll in his hand. . . . .

"Then Balaam, dressed and sitting upon an Ass,[2]— whence the festival took its name, — having spurs upon his heels, is to hold the bridle and spur the ass; a young man with a drawn sword is to stand in the ass's way, and some one creeping under the belly of the ass is to cry out 'Cur me calcaribus miseram sic læditis?' Thereupon an angel speaking to him shall say, 'Desine Regis Balac præceptum perficere.' Voices call to Balaam ; Balaam seems to be prophesying; then Balaam responds, 'Exibit ex Jacob rutilans,' etc." — *Numb.* xxiv. 17.

From the Missal composed for the service of the Feast of the Ass by an Archbishop of Sens, who died

---

[1] "The poet Virgil was introduced singing monkish rhymes, as a Gentile prophet and a translator of the Sibylline oracles." — *Hone's Mysteries and Religious Shows.*

[2] According to Hone the animal was of wood and inclosed a speaker.

in 1222, M. Millin has given an account of a singularly droll ceremony : —

" On the eve of the day appointed for the celebration before vespers, the clergy went in procession to the door of the cathedral, where two choristers sung in a minor key, or rather, squeaking voices : —

> " 'Lux hodie, lux letitiæ, me judice, tristis
> Quisquis erit, removendus erit, solemnibus istis
> Sicut hodie, procul invidiæ, procul omnia mæsta
> Læta volunt, quicumque celibret asinaria festa.'

> " 'Light to-day, the light of joy — I banish every sorrow ;
> Wherever found, be it expelled from our solemnities to-morrow.
> Away be strife and grief and care, from every anxious breast,
> And all be joy and glee in those who keep the Ass's Feast.'

" The anthem being concluded, two canons were deputed to fetch the Ass to the table, where the great chanter sat, to read the order of the ceremonies, and the names of those who were to assist in them. The animal, clad with precious priestly ornaments, was solemnly conducted to the middle of the choir, during which procession a hymn in praise of the Ass was sung in a major key. Its first and last stanzas have been thus Englished : —

> " 'From the country of the East
> Came this strong and handsome beast,
> This able Ass, — beyond compare,
> Heavy loads and packs to bear.
> Huzza, Seignor Ass, Huzza !

> " 'Amen ! bray, most honour'd Ass,
> Sated now with grain and grass ;
> Amen repeat, Amen reply,
> And disregard antiquity.
> Huzza, Seignor Ass, Huzza !'

" The office being in the same style throughout was sung in the most discordant manner possible. The service itself lasted the whole of the night and part of the next day; it was a rhapsody of whatever was sung in the course of the year at the usual church festivals, and formed altogether the strangest and most ridiculous medley imaginable. When the choristers in this long performance were thirsty, wine was unsparingly distributed, and the signal for that part of the ceremony was an anthem commencing ' Conductus ad poculum,'— ' *Brought to the glass.*' ", " The vespers on the second day were ended with an invitation to dinner in the form of an anthem like the rest, ' Conductus ad prandium,'—' *Brought to dinner.*' "

Dr. Douce, F. S. A., says that the earliest mention of the Festum Fatuorum in England is in the reign of Henry IV. The grosser features of it do not appear to have found much favor with the English, whether owing to the good sense or the piety of our forefathers, it does not seem to have long survived the preaching and influence of Wickliffe. Dr. Douce says it was abolished about the end of the fourteenth century.[1]

But the ceremony of the Boy-Bishop in spite of the gross fooleries that had become mixed up with it, survived until the time of Henry VIII. That monarch, influenced doubtless by his animosity to the monks — the chief patrons of these festivals — determined to abolish all such superstitious observances as the cere-

[1] Dr. Douce describes a girdle which tradition reports to have been worn by the Abbot of Fools, in the cathedral of Dijon, on his election into office. It consists of thirty-five square pieces of wood, so contrived as to let into each other, by which means it easily assumes a circular form. On these are carved a variety of ludicrous and grotesque figures, consisting of fools, tumblers, huntsmen, and animals, with others, that from their licentiousness, do not admit of a particular description.

monial of the Boy-Bishop. In a royal proclamation, 1542, the King says : —

"Whereas heretofore dyvers and many superstitious and chyld-ysh observaunces have be used, and yet to this day are observed and kept in many and sundry partes of this realm, as upon Saint Nicho-las, the Holie Innocents, and such like ; children be strangelie decked and apparayled to counterfeit priests, bishops, and women, and be ledde with songes and dances from house to house, blessing the people and gathering of money ; and boyes do singe masse and preach in the pulpitt, with such other unfittinge and inconvenient usages rather to the derysyon than anie true glory of God, or hon-our of his Sayntes: the Kynge's Majestie wylleth and commandeth that henceforth all such superstitious observations be left and clerely extinguished throwout all this realme and dominions," etc.

And yet this " superstitious and chyldysh " observ-ance did not seem so objectionable to the learned and pious Dean Colet, the friend of Erasmus and Sir Thomas More, and one of the most illustrious precur-sors of the English Reformation, for in the statutes of the famous school founded by him (1512) (attached to St. Paul's cathedral), it is ordained that all his scholars " *shall every Childermas day* come to Paulis churche and hear the childe bishop sermon ; and after be at the hygh masse, and each of them offer a 1ᵈ to the childe bysshop, and with them, the maisters and surveyors of the scole."

Perhaps Dean Colet was quite as competent to judge of the expediency of such a ceremony as either the king or his advisers, it being, doubtless, the Dean's in-tention to reform rather than to destroy an ancient

institution.   However, in the reactionary times of
Queen Mary, the proclamation of Henry VIII. was
disregarded.   According to Strype, an edict was issued
November 13, 1554, by the Bishop of London, to all
the clergy of his diocese, to have the procession of a
Boy-Bishop.   And again, " On the 5th of December,
or St. Nicholas Eve, of the same year, ' at *even song*,'
came a commandment that St. Nicholas should not go
abroad or about ; but notwithstanding, it seems, so
much were the citizens taken with the ' *mask* ' of St.
Nicholas (that is, Boy-Bishop), that there went about
these St. Nicholases in divers parishes."

Again, Strype informs us, that " In 1556, on the eve
of his day, St. Nicholas, that is, a boy habited like a
bishop, ' in pontificalibus,' went abroad in most parts
of London, singing after the old fashion, and was received with many ignorant but well-disposed people
into their houses, and had as much good cheer as ever
was wont to be had before, at least in many places."

From this time, St. Nicholas appears to have gone
no more abroad " in pontificalibus," his authority being
now restricted to the castles and halls of the nobility
and gentry, where, in chapels, halls, and kitchens, rival-
ing those of the king himself, the Mock Prelate
transformed into the Christmas Prince continued his
rule " with uncontrolled sway."

Ben Jonson, in his " Masque," presented at court in
1616, has represented such a Lord of Misrule in the
character of Old Father Christmas, attired in round

hose, long stockings, a close doublet, a high-crowned hat, with a broach, a long thin beard, a truncheon, little ruffs, white shoes, his scarfs and garters tied across, and his drum beaten before him.

St. Nicholas now appears as a convert to the principles of the Reformation: " Ha! would you ha' kept me out? Christmas, Old *Christmas, Christmas* of *London*, and Captain *Christmas.* . . . . Why, I am no dangerous Person, and so I told my Friends o' the Guard. I am old *Gregory Christmas* still, and though I come out of *Popes-Head-Alley*, as good a Protestant as any i' my Parish."

Our Boy-Bishop, thus transformed, was now surrounded by a goodly family of children,[1] instead of a chapter of petty Canons as in Pre-Reformation times.

The plea of Protestantism, however, did not satisfy the suspicious Puritanical spirit of that age, for during the civil wars of the seventeenth century, we find him and his children, mince-pie and plum porridge included, solemnly banished the land by Act of Parliament.

But if the Long Parliament could expel him from England, it could not prevent his taking up his abode among the more tolerant Dutch in the " New Netherlands," and there, according to Knickerbocker's " History of New York," " he has continued to flourish at Christmas in spite of the ' Blue Laws ' of the neigh-

---

[1] The names of the children were Misrule, Caroll, Minc'd Pie, Gambol, Post and Pair, New Year's Gift, Mumming, Wassall Offering and Babie-Cocke.

boring Puritanical State of Connecticut." He does not now, however, go any more abroad, habited " in pontificalibus." Having turned Presbyterian, he contents himself with the ordinary guise of a Dutchman, heavily furred, and has also exchanged his wassail-bowl for the " *bowl* " of a short Dutch pipe, with which he has completely mystified and befogged the intellect of his old Puritanical enemies.

CHAPTER VIII.

CHRISTMAS GAMBOLS.

N the gold-en age we are endeavoring to describe, Christmas gambols, and indeed holiday festivities of all kinds were presided over by a " Lord of Misrule," or "Christmas Prince," as he was sometimes termed in Colleges and Inns of Court.

The rights and privileges of this potentate are by some believed to be derived from the Roman Saturna-lia, a festival instituted in commemoration of the freedom and equality which once prevailed on the earth in the golden reign of Saturn.

Faber speaks of them as originating in an old Persico-gothic festival in honor of Buddha; and Purchas, in his " Pilgrimage," as quoted in the Aubrey manuscripts, says, that the custom is deduced from " the Feast in Babylon, kept in honour of the goddess Dorcetha, for five dayes together; during which time the masters were under the dominion of their servants, one of which is usually sett over the rest, and royally cloathed, and was called Sogan, that is, Great Prince."

The ancient Jews, also, had at their merry-making a sort of Lord of Misrule, or "Symposiarch," whose duty it was to promote the general hilarity. " If thou be made the master of the feast," says the author of " Ecclesiasticus," " take diligent care for them, and when thou hast done all thy office, take thy place that thou mayest be merry with them, and receive a crown for thy well ordering of the feast."

But whatever may have been the origin of the office, the authority of the Lord of Misrule was generally acknowledged in England previous to the civil wars of the seventeenth century.

Hollingshed informs us that —

" What time there is alwayes one appointed to make sporte at Courte, called commonly, Lord of Misrule, whose office is not un-knowne to such as have been brought up in nobleman's houses, and among great housekeepers, which use liberal feasting in the season."

Stow says : —

"At the Feast of Christmas, in the king's court, wherever he chanced to reside, there was appointed a Lord of Misrule, or master of merry disports ; the same merry-fellow made his appearance at the house of every nobleman and person of distinction ; and among the rest the Lord Mayor of London, and the sheriffs, had severally of them their Lord of Misrule ; ever contending, without quarrel or offense, who should make the rarest pastimes to delight the beholders ; this pageant potentate began his rule at All-hallow Eve, and continued the same till the morrow after the Feast of the Purification, in which space there were fine and subtle disguisings, masks, and mummeries."

A good idea of the merry-makings of our ancestors, and of the nature of the duties of the Lord of Misrule, or master of ceremonies, may be formed from a consideration of the will of the Right Worshipful Richard Evelyn, Esqr, of the sixteenth century, father of the author of " The Diary," and Deputy-Lieutenant of the counties of Surrey and Sussex, thus appointing and defining the functions of a Christmas Lord of Misrule, over his estate at Wotton : —

"*Imprimis.* — I give free leave to Owen Flood, my trumpeter, gentleman, to be Lord of Misrule of all good orders during the twelve days. And also I give free leave to the said Owen Flood, to command all and every person or persons whatsoever, as well servants as others, to be at his command whensoever he shall sound his trumpet or music, and to do him service, as though I were present myself, at their perils. . . . . I give full power and authority to his lordship to break up all locks, bolts, bars, doors, and latches, and to fling up all doors out of hinges, to come at those who presume to disobey his lordship's commands. God save the king ! "

"Sir Richard's son did not depart from the economy and hospitality of the old house, but '*more veterum*,' kept a Christmas in which they had not fewer than three hundred bumpkins every holiday."

Again : Heath, in his "Flagellum," tells us that it was the custom of Sir Oliver Cromwell [uncle of the Protector], "in the festival of Christmas, to entertain in his house a Master of Misrule or the Revels, to make mirth for the guests, and to direct the dances and the music, and generally all manner of sport and gambols." According to the same authority, "This fellow, Mr. (Oliver) Cromwell, have besmeared his own clothes with filth, accosts in the midst of a frisking dance, and so grimed him and others upon every turn, that such a smell was raised, that the spectators could hardly endure the room. Whereupon the said Master of Misrule, perceiving the matter, caused him to be laid hold on, and by his command to be thrown into a pond adjoining to the house and there to be soused over head and ears, and rinsed of the filth and pollution sticking to him, which was accordingly executed. Sir Oliver suffering his nephew to undergo the punishment of his unmannerly folly."

In pre-Reformation times, this "Master of Merry Disports" held his revels in or about the Church. Then, the nave of the Church was used for a great variety of purposes. Not only were Courts of Justice held in them, but Ales, Faires and Markets periodically took place beneath the vaulted roof of many a stately minster.

Even the clergy in those days might be seen mingling among the busy throng of buyers and sellers, and observing, with at least apparent approval, the gambols of the Morrice dancers, and the stage of the Miracle players; whilst the laity of the day, as they went to Church, could easily combine devotion, business, and amusement.

Strype says, " in many churches, cathedral as well as other, and especially in London, many frays, quarrels, riots, bloodsheddings were committed. They used also commonly to bring horses and mules into and through churches, and shooting off hand guns, making the same which were properly appointed to God's service and common prayer like a stable or common inn, or rather a den and sink of all unchristiness."

Henry VIII. endeavored to reform these abuses, declaring in a proclamation that henceforth no Christian person should abuse the same (*i. e.*, churches), either by eating, drinking, buying, selling, playing, dancing, or with other profane or worldly matters. For all soberness, quietness, and godliness ought there to be used.

Cranmer also endeavored, but in vain, to suppress this irreverent use of churches. Indeed, the abuse complained of was not totally abolished until the civil wars of the seventeenth century, when the troopers of Cromwell overthrew the authority of the Lord of Misrule, or rather in buff coat and bandolier set themselves up in his stead.

In rural England, the doings of these Lords of Misrule have been thus amusingly described by Stubbs, who must have been an eye-witness : —

"First of all, the wilde heads of the parish flocking togither, chuse them a graund captaine of mischiefe, whom they innoble with the title of Lord of Misrule ; and him they crowne with great solemnity, and adopt for their king. This king annoynted chooseth forth twentie, fourty, threescore, or an hundred, lustie guttes, like to himself, to waite upon his lordly majesty, and to guarde his noble person. Then every one of these men he investeth with his liveries of greene, yellow, or some other light wanton colour, and as though they were not gaudy ynaugh, they bedecke themselves with scarffes, ribbons and laces, hanged all over with gold ringes, pretious stones, and other jewels. This done, they tie about either legge twentie, or fourtie belles, with rich handkerchiefes in their handes, and sometimes laide across over their shoulders and neckes, borrowed, for the most part, of their pretie Mopsies and loving Bessies. Thus all thinges set in order, then have they their *hobby*-horses, their dragons, and other antiques, together with their baudie pipers, and thundring drummers to strike up the devils daunce withal. Then march this heathen company towards the church, their pypers pyping, their drummers thundring, their stumpes dauncing, their belles jyngling, their handkerchiefes fluttering aboute their heades like madde men, their *hobby*-horses and other monsters skirmishing amongst the throng : and in this state they go to the church though the minister be at prayer or preaching, dauncing and singing like devils incarnate, with such a confused noise that no man can heare his owne voyce. Then the foolish people they looke, they stare, they laugh, they fleere, and mount upon the formes and pewes, to see these goodly pageants solemnized. Then after this, aboute the church they go againe and againe, and so fourthe into the churche-yard, where they have commonly their summer halls, their bowers, arbours, and banqueting houses

set up, wherein they feaste, banquette, and daunce all that day, and peradventure all that night too ; and thus these terrestrial furies spend the Sabbath-day. Then, for the further innobling of this honourable lordane — lord I should say — they have certaine papers wherein is painted some babelerie or other of imagerie worke, and these they call my Lord of Misrules badges or cognizances. These they give to every one that will give them money to mantaine them in this their heathenish devilrie ; and who will not show himself buxome to them and give them money, they shall be mocked and flouted shamefully ; yea, and many times carried upon a cowlstaffe, and dived over heade and eares in water, or otherwise most horribly abused. And so besotted are some, that they not only give them money, but weare their badges or cognizances in their hattes or cappes openly. Another sorte of fantasticall fooles bring to these hell-hounds, the Lord of Misrule and his complices, some bread, some good ale, some new cheese, some old cheese, some custardes, some cracknels, some cakes, some flauns, some tartes, some creame, some meate, some one thing and some another."

It would seem from the above, although Strutt appears to have inferred in his "Sports and Pastimes" that Stubbs was speaking of the Christmas holidays, that the Lord of Misrule was sometimes also president over the summer sports; and that his authority in some cases must have occasionally extended over the whole period, from All-hallows till Whitsuntide. Stubbs speaks of this revel being on the Sabbath-day, and also of their erecting summer-halls, etc., in the church-yard, from which we may infer that the Sabbath-day mentioned, was a *Whitsunday*, because, the "belles that were tied about either legge," indicate the morris-dance, a dance peculiar to Whitsuntide.

In addition to the Christmas Mummeries noticed in the preceding chapters, a brief account should be given of some of the other games and amusements appropriate to this season.

Amongst the list of Christmas sports, we find " jugglers and jack-puddings, scrambling for nuts and apples, dancing the hobby-horse, hunting owls and squirrels, the fool-plough, hot-cockles, a stick moving on a pivot with an apple at one end and a candle at the other, so that he who missed his bite burned his nose, blindman's buff, forfeits, interludes, and mock plays.

Brand, in his " Popular Antiquities," speaking of these games, says, " I find in a tract entitled ' Round About our Coal-fire,' " or " Christmas Entertainments," published in the early part of the last century, the following : —

"Then comes mumming or masquerading, when the squire's wardrobe is ransacked for dresses of all kinds. Corks are burnt to black the faces of the fair, or make deputy mustachios, and every one of the family, except the squire himself, must be transformed."

This account further says : —

"The time of the year being cold and frosty, the diversions are within doors, either in exercise, or by the fireside. Dancing is one of the chief exercises ; or else there is a match at Blindman's Buff or Puss in the Corner. The next game is Questions and Commands, when the commander may oblige his subjects to answer any lawful question, and make the same obey him instantly, under the penalty of being smutted, or paying such forfeit as may be laid on the aggressor. Most of the other diversions are cards and dice."

Although there appears to have been a considerable falling off in modern times in the number and variety of these Christmas games and amusements, still we gather from the above that the sports on a Christmas Eve, a hundred and fifty years ago, were not very much unlike those at present in vogue. The names of almost all the pastimes above mentioned must be familiar to every reader, who has probably participated in some of them. One of these favorite Christmas sports, once generally played on Christmas Eve, has been handed down to us from time immemorial, under the name of Snap-Dragon. In England this amusement is still very popular, but as it is not so well known elsewhere, we subjoin from the " Book of Days," a description of the game: —

"A quantity of raisins is deposited in a large bowl or dish (the broader and shallower this is, the better), and brandy or some other spirit is poured over the fruit and ignited. The by-standers now endeavor, by turns, to grasp a raisin, by plunging their hands through the flames ; and as this is somewhat of an arduous feat, requiring both courage and rapidity of action, a considerable amount of laughter and merriment is evoked at the expense of the unsuccessful competitors. As an appropriate accompaniment we introduce here —

"THE SONG OF SNAP-DRAGON.

" ' Here he comes with flaming bowl,
Don't he mean to take his toll,
Snip ! Snap ! Dragon !

" ' Take care you don't take too much,
Be not greedy in your clutch,
           Snip ! Snap ! Dragon !

" ' With his blue and lapping tongue
Many of you will be stung,
           Snip ! Snap ! Dragon !

" ' For he snaps at all that comes
Snatching at his feast of plums,
           Snip ! Snap ! Dragon !

" ' But old Christmas makes him come,
Though he looks so fee ! fa ! fum !
           Snip ! Snap ! Dragon !

" ' Don't'ee fear him — be but bold —
Out he goes, his flames are cold,
           Snip ! Snap ! Dragon !

"While the sport of Snap-dragon is going on, it is usual to extinguish all the lights in the room, so that the lurid glare from the flaming spirits may exercise to the full its weird-like effect."

NOTE. — "Burton, in his 'Anatomy of Melancholy' mentions as the winter amusements of his day — 'Cardes, tables, and dice, shovelboard, chesse-play, the philosopher's game, small trunkes, shuttlecocke, billiards, musicke, masks, singing, dancing, ule-games, frolicks, jests, riddles, catches, purposes, questions and commands, merry tales of errant knights, queenes, lovers, lords, ladies, giants, dwarfes, theeves, cheaters, witches, fayries, goblins, friers, etc.' "

CHAPTER IX.

THE CHRISTMAS PRINCE.

E turn now from country sports and pastimes to the consideration of the more splendid and elaborate doings of the town — for it is in the Universities and Inns of Court, rather than in the rural districts of England, that we find the Lord of Misrule assuming a state and dignity which astonishes people living in this nineteenth century of ours.

Amongst the more powerful Nobles, this Lord of Misrule, — " Barne Bishop " or " Abbot of Unreason," was sometimes styled " Master of the Revels," in imitation of the royal establishments, where there was formerly a permanent and distinguished officer of that name. But in the Colleges of the Universities and in the Inns of Court, this " Master of Merry Disports," who was elected from among themselves for his wit and ingenuity, was commonly dignified with a title more appropriate to the great authority with which he was invested; namely, that of " Christmas Prince," or sometimes " King of Christmas."

Various old authors have left us interesting accounts of the doings of these Christmas potentates. In 1561, a Christmas Prince, having with him a train of one hundred horsemen, richly appareled, rode through London to the Inner Temple, where there was great reveling throughout the Christmas. Lord Robert Dudley, afterwards Earl of Leicester, being the constable and marshal, under the name of Palaphilos, and Christopher Hatton, afterwards Chancellor, master of the game. A sort of Parliament had been previously held on St. Thomas's Eve, to decide whether the society should keep Christmas, and if so the oldest bencher should deliver a speech on the occasion, and the oldest butler publish the officers' names, and then —" in token of joy and good liking, the bench and company pass beneath the hearth, and sing a carol, and so to *boyer* " (collation).

Jeaffreson, in his book about these Lawyers, has given a vivid description of this scene, derived from Gerard Leigh and Dugdale.

Palaphilos, the Christmas Prince, was dressed in a " complete suit of elaborately wrought and richly gilt armor ; he bore above his helmet a cloud of curiously dyed feathers and held a gilt pole-axe in his hand. By his side walked the Lieutenant of the Tower (Mr. Parker) clad in white armor, and like Palaphilos, furnished with feathers and a pole-axe." On entering the hall, the Prince and his Lieutenant were preceded by sixteen trumpeters, four drummers, and a company of fifers, followed by four halberdiers in white armor. The procession marched three times round the fire that blazed in the centre of the hall. After Prince Palaphilos had taken his seat at the invitation of the mock Lord Chancellor, " Kit Hatton (as Master of the Game) entered the hall, dressed in a complete suit of green velvet, and holding a green bow in his left hand. His quiver was supplied with green arrows, and round his neck was slung a hunting horn. By Kit's side arrayed in exactly the same style, walked the Ranger of the Forests (Mr. Martyn); and having forced their way into the crowded chamber, the two young men blew three blasts of venery upon their horns, and then paced three times round the fire. After thus parading the hall, they paused before the Lord Chancellor, to whom the Master of Game made three curtsies, and then, on his knees, proclaimed the desire of his heart to serve the mighty Prince Palaphilos. Having risen from his kneeling posture, Kit Hatton blew his horn, and at the signal his huntsman entered the room, bringing with him a fox, a cat, and ten couples of hounds. Forthwith the fox was released from the pole to which it was bound; and when the luckless creature had crept into a corner under one of the tables, the ten couples of hounds were sent in pursuit . . . . Over tables and under tables, up the hall and down the hall, those score hounds went at full cry after a miserable fox, which they eventually ran into and killed in the cinder-pit, or as Dugdale expresses it, 'beneath the fire.' That work achieved, the cat was turned off and the hounds sent after her," etc.

This singular hunt seems at one time to have been general in great houses, and to have had a sort of symbolic signification. What that was before the Reformation does not appear, but " In ane compendious Boke of godly and spiritual Songs, Edinburgh, 1621, printed from an old copy," are the following lines, seemingly referring to some such pageant : —

> " The hunter is Christ that hunts in haist,
> The hunds are Peter and Pawle,
> The Paip is the fox, Rome is the rox,
> That rubbis us on the gall."

Scarcely less out of place in the dining room than Kit Hatton's hounds, was the mule, fairly mounted, on which the Prince Palaphilos made his appearance at the High Table after Supper, when he notified to his subjects in what manner they were to disport themselves till bed-time.

There was also, it appears, a very splendid Christmas at the Middle Temple in 1635, when Mr. Francis Vivian of Cornwall was the Christmas Prince, and expended £2,000 out of his own pocket, beyond the allowance of the society, in order to support his state with sufficient dignity.

"The Middle Temple House," writes the Rev. G. Garrard to the Earl of Strafford, January 8, 1635 : —

" Have set up a prince, who carries himself in great state. . . . . He hath all his great officers attending him, lord keeper, lord treasurer, eight white staves at the least, captain of his pensioners, captain of his guard, two chaplains, who on Sunday last preached before him, and in the pulpit made three low legs to his excellency before they began, which is much laughed at. My Lord Chamberlain lent him two fair cloths of state, one hung up in the hall, under which he dines, the other in his privy chamber ; he is served on the knee, and all that come to see him kiss his hand on their knee. My Lord of Salisbury hath sent him pole-axes for his pensioners. He sent to my Lord of Holland, his justice in Eyre, for venison, which he willingly sends him, to the Lord Mayor and Sheriffs of London for wine, all obey. Twelfth-Day was a great day, going to the chapel many petitions were delivered him, which he gave to his masters of the requests. He hath a favorite, whom with some others, gentlemen of great quality, he knighted as he returned from church, and dined in great state."

In the early part of the Eighteenth Century these revels ceased, having gradually fallen off; and the dignity of Master of the Revels, instead of being eagerly sought for, as in former times, required a premium to induce any member to take it upon him.

The expense of maintaining the mock court of the Christmas Prince was indeed very great, a short reign of forty days proving often ruinous to ambitious gentlemen resident in the Inns of Court.

In the Universities, where the expenses were on a much more economical scale than those in London, the dignity of the office could not be properly maintained without contributions levied on the willing subjects of the Mock Prince. At the memorable Christmas observed at St. John's College,[1] Oxford, in 1607, this method of replenishing the royal exchequer was resorted to. The supplies thus obtained were expended in revels and dramatic entertainments similar to those performed by the Lawyers at the Inns of Court.

It might be well to give here by way of caution an extract from the account of the Oxford Christmas Prince, lest any one in these antiquity-loving days should be disposed to revive such sports and pastimes as those above referred to.

Says the Chronicler:

" Let others herafter take heed how they attempte the like, vnlesse they find better meanes at home, and better mindes abroad."
. . . . " Wee intended in these exercises the practise and audacity of our youth, the creditt and good name of our Colledge, the love and favor of the vniuersity ; but instead of all these (so easie a

[1] See Appendix.

thing it is to be deceived in a good meaning) wee met with peevish-
nesse at home, peruersnes abroad, contradictiones everywhere ; some
neuer thought themselves entreated enough to their owne good and
creditt ; others thought themselves able to doe nothing if they could
not thwarte and hinder something ; most stood by and gave aime,
willing to see much and doe nothing, nay pchaunce they were ready
to procure most trouble, which would bee sure to yeild least helpe.
And yet wee may not so much grudge at faults at home as wee may
justly complaine of hard measure abroad ; for insteed of the love and
favor of the vniuersitie, wee found oʳ selves (wee will say justly) taxed
for any the least errour, [though ingenious spirits would have
pdoned many things, where all things were entended for their owne
pleasure] but most vnjustly censured and envied for that wᶜʰ was
done [wee dare say] indifferently well : so that, in a word wee paid
deere for trouble, and in a manner hired and sent for men to
doe vs wrong."

It is difficult for us now to realize the extent to which
these Christmas Gambols were carried, down even to
the end of the seventeenth century. Whitelocke, the
friend of Cromwell and once Speaker of the House of
Commons, President of the Council of State, and also
Keeper of the Great Seal, and other eminent lawyers,
statesmen, and philosophers of his time, prided themselves not a little on their taste and skill, as well as on
the authority exercised by them.

Whitelocke has left on record a curious account of
his own princely doings at the Christmas revels held at
the Temple in 1629. In his twenty-fourth year, he was
unanimously chosen Master of the Revels by the
young gentlemen of the Middle Temple. "The company was about twenty in number, and they met nearly

7

every evening at St. Dunstan's tavern, in a large new room, called the 'Oracle of Apollo'; each member brought friends with him, when he thought fit, provided there was no secret sitting specially appointed for discussing 'ways and means.' In this hall they held, after their sage consultations, both solemn dinners and sober suppers, for not one among them was ever seen to be drunk, and not one of them was ever guilty of debauchery during that whole winter's season." The meetings were, in short, a kind of miniature parliament of which Whitelocke was the speaker. Besides voting supplies, the weighty business to be transacted there, was "to practise their dancing, to exercise both their wits and bodies; not to cloud their reason or parts with excess or debauchery, but to improve their judgment and by good discourse and conversation; sometimes by putting of cases; and they did appear together much more like to grave ancients in a council chamber than to young revellers in a house of drinking." The dancing itself was a very grave ceremony, as the reader will perceive; for at All-hallows day (November 1), which the Templars considered the beginning of Christmas, the Master, as soon as the evening was come, entered the hall, followed by sixteen revellers. They were proper, handsome young gentlemen, habited in rich suits, shoes and stockings, hats and great feathers. The Master led them in his bar-gown, with a white staff in his hand, the music playing before them. They began with the old masques; after that they danced the Brawl, and then the Master took his seat whilst the revellers flaunted through galliards, corantos, French and country dances, till it grew very late. As might be expected, the reputation of this dancing soon brought a store of other gentlemen and ladies, some of whom were of great quality; and when the ball was over, the festive party adjourned to Sir Sidney Montague's chamber, lent for the purpose to our young president. At length, the court ladies and grandees were allured, — to the contentment of his (Whitelocke's) vanity it may have been, but entailing on him serious expense, — and then there was great striving for places to see them on the part of the London citizens. . . . . To crown the ambition and vanity of all, a great German lord had a desire to witness the revels, then making such a sensation at court, and the Templars entertained him at great cost to themselves, receiving in exchange that which cost the great noble very little, — his avowal that ' Dere was no such nople gollege in Ghristendom as deirs.' "

Perhaps of all the splendid festivities recorded for the admiration of posterity, that which concluded the Christmas Holiday season of 1633 is the most remarkable, indeed it was the last great masque presented to Charles I. A very full and graphic account of it is given by Whitelocke in his " Memoirs."

The following summary of the proceeding is taken from Jeaffreson's " Book about Lawyers : "—

" The masque was entitled the ' Triumph of Peace,' and was written by Shirley ; it was produced with a pomp and lavish expenditure that were without precedent. The organization and guidance of the undertaking were entrusted to a committee of eight barresters, two from each of the four Inns of Court. . . . . The committee of management had their quarters at Ely House, Holborn, and from that historic palace the masquers started for Whitehall on the eve of Candlemas Day, 1633–1634.

"It was a superb procession. First, marched twenty tall footmen blazing in liveries of scarlet cloth trimmed with lace, each of them holding a baton in his right hand, and in his left a flaring torch that covered his face with light, and made the steel and silver of his sword-scabbard shine brilliantly. A company of the marshal's men marched next with firm and even steps, clearing the way for their master. A burst of deafening applause came from the multitude as the marshal rode through the gateway of Ely House, and caracoled over the Holborn way on the finest charger that the king's stables could furnish. A perfect horseman and the handsomest man then in town, Mr. Darrel of Lincoln's Inn, had been elected to the office of marshal in deference to his wealth, his noble aspect, his fine nature, and his perfect mastery of all manly sports. On either side of Mr. Darrel's horse marched a lacquey bearing a flambeau, and the marshal's page was in attendance with his master's cloak. An interval of some twenty paces, and then came the marshal's body guard, composed of one hundred mounted gentlemen of the Inns of Court — twenty-five from each house ; showing in their faces the signs of gentle birth and honorable nurture ; and with strong hands reining mettlesome chargers that had been furnished for their use by the greatest nobles of the land. This flood of flashing chivalry was succeeded by an anti-masque of beggars and cripples, mounted on the lamest, and most unsightly of rat-tailed screws and spavined ponies, and wearing dresses that threw derision on legal vestments and decorations. Another anti-masque satirized the wild projects of crazy speculators and inventors ; and as it moved along the spectators laughed aloud at the ' fish-call,' or looking-glass for fishes in the sea, very useful for fishermen to call all kinds of fish to their nets.' The newly invented wind-mate for raising a breeze over becalmed seas, the 'movable hydraulic' which should give sleep to patients suffering under fever.

"Chariots and horsemen, torch-bearers and lacqueys, followed in order. 'Then came the first chariot of the grand masquers, which was not so large as those that went before, but most curiously framed, carved, and painted with exquisite art, and purposely for this service and occasion. The form of it was after that of the Roman triumphant chariots. The seats in it were made of oval form in the back end of the chariot, so that there was no precedence in them and the face of all that sat in it might be seen together. The colors of the first chariot were silver and crimson, given by the lot to Gray's Inn; the chariot was drawn with four horses all abreast, and they were covered to their heels all over with cloth of tissue, of the colors of crimson and silver, huge plumes of white and red feathers on their heads; the coachman's cap and feather, his long coat, and his very whip and cushion of the same stuff and color. In this chariot sat the four grand masquers of Gray's Inn, their habits, doublets, trunk-hose, and caps of most rich cloth of tissue, and wrought as thick with silver spangles as they could be placed; large white stockings up to their trunk-hose, and rich sprigs in their caps, themselves proper and beautiful young gentlemen. On each side of the chariot were four footmen in liveries of the color of the chariot, carrying huge flamboys in their hands, which with the torches, gave such a lustre to the paintings, spangles, and habits that hardly anything could be invented to appear more glorious.' Six musicians followed the state chariots of Gray's Inn, playing as they went; and then came the triumphal cars of the Middle Templars, the Inner Templars, and the Lincoln's Inn men, each car being drawn by four horses and attended by torch-bearers, flambeau-bearers, and musicians. In shape these four cars were alike, but they differed in the color of their fittings. Whilst Gray's Inn used scarlet and silver, the Middle Templars chose blue and silver decorations, and each of the other two houses adopted a distinctive color for the housings of their horses and the liveries of their servants. . . . . Through the illuminated streets this pageant marched to the sound of trumpets and drums, cymbals and fifes, amidst the deafening acclamations of the delighted town ; and when the lawyers reached White-hall, the king and queen were so delighted with the spectacle, that the procession was ordered to make the circuit of the tilt-yard for the gratification of their Majesties, who would fain see the sight once again from a window of the palace (the very window through which the king was conducted fifteen years after to the stage of the scaffold)."

" Is there need to speak of the manner in which the masque was acted, of the music and dances, of the properties and scenes, of the stately banquet after the play, and the grand ball which began at a still later hour, of the king's urbanity and the graciousness of Henrietta, who ' did the honor to some of the masquers to dance with them herself, and to judge them as good dancers as she ever saw.' "

Besides the charge for the music, the cost of the dresses of the horsemen, and the liveries of their pages and lacqueys, the expense of the masque was found to exceed £20,000, which had to be borne by the societies of the Inns of Court, and by some of the wealthier members individually.

Says Whitelocke, at the conclusion of his account of this grand masque : " Thus these dreams past, and these pomps vanished."

But the sad and sober days of the Commonwealth came when Christmas was solemnly banished the land by Act of Parliament. Needham, lamenting this sad change, says : —

"Gone are those golden days of yore,
　When Christmas was a High Day :
Whose sports we now shall see no more —
　'T is turned into Good Friday."

The parliamentary order referred to enjoined that
" the twenty-fifth of December should be strictly observed as a fast, and that all men should pass it in
humbly bemoaning the great national sin which they
and their fathers had so often committed on that day
by romping under the mistletoe, eating boar's head,
and drinking ale flavored with roasted apples." No
public act of that time, says Lord Macaulay,[1] seems to
have irritated the people more. " On the next anniversary of the festival formidable riots broke out in many
places. The constables were resisted, the magistrates
insulted, the houses of noted zealots attacked, and the
proscribed service of the day openly read in the
churches."

[1] By the way, Lord Macaulay is particularly eloquent in his defense of the festival condemned by the puritanical parliament of 1644 : " Christmas had been
from time immemorial, the season of joy and domestic affection, the season when
families assembled, when children came home from school, when quarrels were
made up, when carols were heard in every street, when every house was decorated
with evergreens, and every table was loaded with good cheer. At that season all
hearts, not utterly destitute of kindness were enlarged and softened. At that season the poor were admitted to partake largely of the overflowings of the wealth
of the rich, whose bounty was peculiarly acceptable on account of the shortness
of the days and the severity of the weather. At that season the interval between
landlord and tenant, master and servant, was less marked than through the rest
of the year. Where there is much enjoyment, there will be some excess ; yet, on
the whole, the spirit in which the holiday was kept was not unworthy of a Christian festival."

At the Restoration of Charles II., there was a partial revival of the Christmas Gambols, together with the May Games or Sports and Pastimes that had been forbidden by the Long Parliament.

In the eighteenth century the Inns of Court revels, which had for so many generations been conspicuous amongst the gayeties of the town, became less and less magnificent; dying out altogether in the time of the unappreciative George the Second.

NOTE. — "In 1697–8 Peter the Great was a guest at the Christmas revels of the Templars. On that occasion the Czar enjoyed a favorable opportunity for gratifying his love of strong drink, and for witnessing the ease with which our ancestors drank wine by the magnum and punch by the gallon, when they were bent upon enjoyment." — *Book about Lawyers.*

CHAPTER X.

HE custom of serving the boar's head with minstrelsy at the Christmas dinner, with more or less of the ceremonies still used at Queen's College, Oxford, was very general in England previous to the civil wars of the seventeenth century, not only in the halls of the Universities, but also in the houses of the nobility and gentry. According to Aubrey,—"The first dish that was served up in the old baronial halls, was the boar's head, which was brought in with great state, and with minstrelsy; and between the flourishes of the heralds' trumpets, carols were chanted forth."

Perhaps the most splendid example of Christmas banqueting of this kind of which we have read, is that recently illustrated by Gilbert, which took place in the reign of Henry VII., in the great hall of Westminster. To this feast the Mayor and Aldermen of London were invited, and all the sports of the time were exhibited before them in the great hall, which was hung with tapestry; "which sports being ended *in the morning*, the King, Queen, and Court sat down at a table of stone, to one hundred and twenty dishes, placed by as many knights and esquires; while the Mayor was served with twenty-four dishes and abundance of wine. And finally, the King and Queen being conveyed with great lights into the palace, the Mayor with his company, in barges, returned to London by break of next day."

It is this royal Christmas which Mr. Gilbert has represented with such truthfulness. The artist has selected the upper end of the hall, showing the great stone table, with the King and Queen seated beneath a canopy of state, emblazoned with the royal arms; the dais wall is hung with tapestry, and wreathed with Christmas evergreens, and the banners above are surmounted with laurel crowns. The servitors are bringing in the royal dishes, conspicuous amongst which

is the peacock in all its glory of gaudy plumage, and
the boar's head dressed with holly, bay, and rosemary.
The following celebrated account of a Christmas dinner, at the time of the famous "Christmas Prince" who
presided over the festivities at St. John's, Oxford, in
1607, is taken from the "Miscellanea Antiqua Anglicana": —

"At diner beinge sett downe in ye Hall at ye high table in y^e
Vice Præsident's place [for ye Præsident himself was then allso
p'sent] hee was serued wth 20 dishes to a messe, all wch were
brought in by Gentlemen of ye Howse attired in his Guard's coats,
vshered in by ye L^{rd} Comptroller and other Officers of ye Hall.

"The first messe was a Boar's head, wch was carried by the tallest
and lustiest of all ye Guard, before whom (as attendants) wente first,
one attired in a horseman's coate, wth a Boares-speare in his hande ;
next to him another Huntsman in greene wth a bloody faulcion
drawne ; next to him 2 Pages in tafatye sarcenet, each of y^{em} wth a
messe of mustard ; next to whome came hee y^t carried ye Boar's
head crost wth a greene silke Scarfe, by wch hunge ye empty Scab-
bard of the faulcion wch was carried before him. As y^{et} entered y^e
Hall, He sange this Christmas Caroll ye three last verses [lines]
of euerie Staffe being repeated after him by the whole companye : " —

> "The Boare is dead,
>   Loe, heare is his head,
>   What man could haue done more
>   Then his head of to strike
>   Meleager like,
>   And bringe it as I doe before?

> "He liuinge spoyled
>   Where good men toyled,
>   Which made kinde Ceres sorrye ;

But now dead and drawne,
Is very good brawne,
And wee haue brought it for y^u.

"Then sett downe ye Swineyard
The foe to ye Vineyard
Lett Bacchus crowne his fall,
Lett this Boares-head and mustard
Stand for Pigg, Goose and Custard,
And so y^u are wellcome all."

The ceremony still observed in Queen's College, Oxford, differs but little from the above. The custom has probably been observed since the foundation of the college in 1340. The Boar's Head,[1] highly decorated with bay, holly, rosemary, etc., in a large pewter dish, is slowly borne into the hall by two strong servants of the college, who hold it up as high as they can, that it may be seen by the visitors ranged on either side of the hall. The gentleman who sings the ancient carol, or "Boar's Head Song" (generally one of the members of the college, though sometimes one of the choir of Magdalen College), immediately precedes the Boar's Head, and as he commences the song with, "The Boar's Head in

---

[1] Brawn, decorated with bay and rosemary, has been substituted for the Boar's head. The following traditional receipt we give as we had it from an English lady. "*Brawn.* — Take a pig's head and soak in salt and water all night, scrape and well clean the head, removing the brains and eyes. Boil until tender enough to take the bones out easily. When quite tender pick the meat from the bones and chop fine, seasoning to your taste, with red and black pepper, cloves, mace, nutmeg, and salt ; mix well together and put in a press. Let it remain until cold."

hand bear I," touches the dish with his right hand. Two young choristers from Magdalen College follow, to sing conjointly with many of the junior members of Queen's College, the chorus, " Caput apri defero," etc.[1] The dish is carried as before stated, to the high table, where sit the Provost, Bursar, Fellows, and others, and at which many visitors are congregated.

The places where *now* the boar's head ceremony is specially observed, by bringing in the gigantic dish in procession, with song and chorus, on Christmas Day, are Queen's College, Oxford ; St. John's College, Cambridge ; and the Inner Temple, London.

There has been also, elsewhere, and even in this country, successful attempts at a revival of this ancient ceremony. At the opening of the New Rooms of the Century Club of New York, on Twelfth-Night, 1858, there was a pageant similar in character. The ceremonies on the occasion were like those enacted in the Inns of Court, in the sixteenth and seventeenth centuries. The writer was told by those who were present that everything was done according to ancient custom, the decorations of the spacious apartments and the costumes were very picturesque, and the ancient cookery decidedly good.

There was also in 1865, at Troy, N. Y., a similar serving up of the boar's head with minstrelsy, at a Christmas dinner, in the school-room of the Mary Warren Free Institute. The choir sang in procession

---

[1] For Carol, see Appendix.

the appropriate carol; the first bass, with his hand on
the silver dish chanting the solo, —

> The boar's head in hand bear I,
> Bedecked with bay and rosemary,
> And I pray you, my masters, be merry,
> Quot estis in convivio.

The schoolroom with its arched fireplace and blazing yule-log presented quite the appearance of an antique baronial hall.

Various accounts have been given of the origin of
this ancient custom of bringing in the boar's head. By
some it is said to have originated with the Romans,
who served up the wild boar, sometimes in parts, and
sometimes the entire animal, as the first dish at their
feasts.

The boar's head was also an established Yule-tide
dish of the North in the old heathen times. The
whole boar and boar's head, gorgeously ornamented,
gilt, and painted, was also a favorite festival dish in
England during the Norman era. Perhaps, as the
wild boar was anciently accounted a public enemy,
ferocious and destructive, a successful encounter with
him was in those days considered an achievement
worthy the valor of an accomplished knight, entitling
him to the gratitude of the country. An old carol
from Mr. Wright's MS. seems to confirm this supposition : —

" Tidings I bring you for to tell
  What in wild forest me befell,
  When I in with a wild beast fell,
    With a boar so bryme " (fierce).

" A boar so bryme that me pursued,
  Me for to kill so sharply moved,
  That brymly beast so cruel and rude,
    There tamed I him,
  And reft from him both life and limb.

" Truly, to show you this is true,
  His head I with my sword did hew,
  To make this day new mirth for you,
    Now eat thereof anon.

" Eat, and much good do it you,
  Take your bread and mustard thereto ;
  Joy with me, that this I have done,
  I pray you be glad every one,
    And all rejoice as one."

The curious custom called the " Rhyne Toll of
Chetwode Manor," may be also cited by way of illustration. The tradition is, that at a very early period
of English history, a lord of Chetwode, the ancestor
of the present proprietor, slew in single combat an
enormous wild boar, the terror of the surrounding
country. For this good service, he and his heirs had
conferred on them by royal authority certain valuable
manorial rights and privileges, which the family enjoy
to this day. An old ballad modernized thus commemorates the deed : —

" Then he blowed a blast full North, South, East, and West —
　　Wind well thy horn good hunter ! —
And the wild boar then heard him full in his den,
　　As he was a jovial hunter.

" Then he made the best of his speed unto him —
　　Wind well thy horn good hunter ! —
Swift flew the boar, with his tusks smear'd with gore,
　　To Sir Ryalas, the jovial hunter.
" Then the wild boar, being so stout and strong —
　　Wind well thy horn good hunter ! —
Thrash'd down the trees as he ramped him along,
　　To Sir Ryalas, the jovial hunter.

Then they fought four hours in a long summer day —
　　Wind well thy horn good hunter ! —
Till the wild boar fain would have got him away
　　From Sir Ryalas, the jovial hunter.

" When Sir Ryalas he drawed his broadsword with might -
　　Wind well thy horn good hunter ! —
And he fairly cut the boar's head off quite,
　　For he was a jovial hunter."

This tradition (thus commemorated) received, about
half a century since, a remarkable confirmation. Within
a mile of Chetwode Manor house there existed a large
mound, surrounded by a ditch, and bearing the name
of the " Boar's Pond." About the year 1810, the tenant to whose farm it belonged, wishing to bring it into
cultivation, began to fill up the ditch by leveling the
mound, when having lowered the latter about four
feet, he came on the skeleton of an enormous boar,

lying flat on its side, and at full length. The field containing it is still called the Boar's Head Field.[1]

There is, however, a very different account of the origin of the custom of serving the boar's head at Christmas, given by Dean Wade, in his " Walks about Oxford " : —

"Tradition presents this usage as a commemoration of an act of valor, performed by a student of a college, who, walking in the neighboring forest of Shotover, and reading ' Aristotle,' was suddenly attacked by a wild boar. The furious beast came open-mouthed upon the youth, who, however, very courageously and with a happy presence of mind, is said to have rammed in the volume and cried, ' *Græcum est* ' (it is Greek); fairly," adds the Dean, " choking the savage with the sage."

Perhaps this manner of disposing of two enemies at once was considered by the Oxonians of that day an event worthy of a particular commemoration ; the Greek philosopher, in their estimation, being the most dreadful *bore* of the two. But whether or not the modern philosophy which succeeded that of Aristotle in this University derived its name " Baconian " from this combat, has not, it appears, been yet decided. Possibly the youth mentioned by the Dean may have acquired the surname of " Bacon " from this exploit, and so transmitted it to posterity with the " inductive " or " Baconian system." The crest of Lord Bacon — the wild boar passant — with the motto " *mediocria firma* " seems to indicate something of the kind.

[1] See Chambers' *Book of Days.*

8

However, the valorous exploit was commemorated by the patron of the student in a stained glass window in Horspath Church, near Shotover. A taberdar,[1] an officer peculiar to Queen's College, is there represented holding on a spear the head of the boar he had slain.

But to return to the subject of the banquet. The dinner would have been thought very incomplete without the appearance of another famous dish peculiar to the season — the Christmas pie — which like the boar's head was anciently served with minstrelsy.

This dainty dish fit " to set before a king," was quite a bill of fare in itself, — fish, flesh, and fowl were to be found beneath its ample crust. We read that, " In the 26th Henry III., the Sheriff of Gloucester was ordered by that monarch to procure twenty salmon to be put into pies at Christmas ; and the Sheriff of Sussex, ten brawns, ten peacocks, and other items for the

---

1 "Taberdars are officers peculiar (it is said) to Queen's College ; their duties appertained to the refectorium, or dining-hall. One of these students in office, in earlier centuries, was returning home through Shotover Forest, after a day spent in recreation, and for safety against wild things, he carried a spear. Jogging homeward leisurely, it pleased him to lull the distance with a page or two of the MS. Aristotle, which he had slung in the folds of his vestment. Thus occupied, and all insecure from foes, biped or quadruped, he was terrified to find that a savage boar was at that instant thrusting itself offensively in his path. The scholar suddenly halted. The boar did likewise. The scholar extended his jaws to raise an alarming cry, and the boar followed the example. Pursuing his advantage, — the man who could study Aristotle in those days was not likely to be blamed for stupidity, — as quick as speech the taberdar thrust the volume, vellum, brass, and all, into the animal's throat, and then finished the business with the spear, whilst his opponent was digesting his classics.

"The scholar's patron commemorated the event in the windows of Horspath Church." — *Wanderings of a Pen and Pencil.*

same purpose." The peacock was only produced at solemn and chivalric banquets, such as that of Christmas, and when thus served up, with gilded beak and plumed crest, his head appearing at one end of the pie, and his tail at the other, spread out in all its glory, was carried in state into the hall to the sound of minstrelsy, by the lady most distinguished for birth and beauty, the other ladies following in due order.

Some of the dishes of the olden time do not appear to us to be very inviting; yet others have stood the test of ages, as we see in the instance of a Christmas-pie, the receipt to make which is preserved in the books of the Salters' Company, in London : —

"For to make a moost choyce Paaste of Gamys to be eten at ye Feste of Chrystemasse (17th Richard II. A. D. 1394)."

A pie so made by the Company's cook in 1836, was found excellent. It consisted of a pheasant, hare, and capon; two partridges, two pigeons, and two rabbits; all boned and put into paste in the shape of a bird, with the livers and hearts, two mutton kidneys, forcemeats, and egg-balls, seasoning, spice, catsup, and pickled mushrooms, filled up with gravy made from the various bones.

The North of England in more modern times continued to maintain a reputation for its Christmas-pies, composed of birds and game. In the "Newcastle Chronicle" of January 6, 1770, there is a description of a giant of this race : —

"On Monday last was brought from Howick to Berwick, to be shipped for London, for Sir Henry Grey, Bart., a pie, the contents whereof are as follows, viz. : 2 bushels of flour, 20 lbs. of butter, 4 geese, 2 turkies, 2 rabbits, 4 wild ducks, 2 woodcocks, 6 snipes, and 4 partridges, 2 neats' tongues, 2 curlews, 7 blackbirds, and 6 pigeons. It is supposed this very great curiosity was made by Mrs. Dorothy Patterson, housekeeper at Howick. It is near nine feet in circumference at bottom, weighs about 12 stone ; will take two men to present it to table ; it is neatly fitted with a case and four small wheels to facilitate its use to every guest that inclines to partake of its contents at table."

The Christmas pie in these days has come to be known as *mince pie*, the term, according to the learned Dr. Parr, having been given to it by the Puritans in derision.

Anciently this pie was baked in the form of a *crache* or *manger*, the crossed bands at the top being traditionally considered to resemble the manner in which a child is secured in its crib. Its various savory contents had, it is supposed, some reference to the offerings of the Magi. Indeed, our mince pie has laid the whole world under contribution : the East and West Indies furnishing the spices and sugar ; Greece and Malaga their currants and raisins ; the North its choicest fruit, and the South pouring over the whole its costliest wine.

In the seventeenth century, the eating of this pie became a test of orthodoxy· Bunyan, when in confinement, and in distress for a comfortable meal, is said to have refused to injure his morals by eating it, the Puritans of his day holding it to be an abomination : —

> " The high-shoe lords of Cromwell's making
> Were not for dainties — roasting, baking ;
> The chiefest food they found most good in
> Was rusty bacon and bag-pudding ;
> Plum-broth was 'Popish,' and mince-pie —
> O, that was flat idolatry ! " —
>
> *Poor Robin's Almanack*, 1685.

There is a superstition in regard to these pies worthy of notice. It is said that in as many different houses as you eat *mince-pie* at Christmas, so many happy months will you have during the ensuing year. Now, as there are just twelve days of Christmas, an enterprising diner-out may thus secure twelve happy months for the New Year.

CHAPTER XI.

N the primitive
Church the Feast
of the Nativity appears
to have been observed
by the Eastern and
Western Churches on
different days. The
Oriental Church keep-
ing it on the 6th of Jan-
uary, calling it the
Epiphany,[1] and the Western Church, from the earliest

---

[1] According to the change of the style (made in England by act of Parliament, 1752), "Old Christmas Day," as it is called, in contradistinction to that of the

time, on the 25th of December. Bingham says that this day was kept as our Saviour's birthday for several ages by the churches of Egypt, Jerusalem, Antioch, Cyprus, and other churches of the East. In the fourth century, Chrysostom, in one of his homilies to the people of Antioch, tells them that — " Ten years were not yet passed since they came to the true knowledge of the day of Christ's birth, which they kept before on Epiphany, till the Western Church gave them better information." From that time it appears that the Nativity and Epiphany were kept as distinct festivals. Both Cassian and Jerome say : —

" The Nativity and Epiphany were kept on different days in all the Western Churches, and both these were indifferently called *Theophania et Epiphania, et prima et secunda Nativitas*, — the ' Epiphany ' or ' Manifestation of God,' and his first and second Nativity ; that being the first, whereon he was born in the flesh, and that his second Nativity, or Epiphany, whereon he was baptized, and manifested by a star to the Gentiles."

In the fourth century, however, the Easterns changed their festival of the Nativity, and united with the Westerns in observing the 25th of December. This variation in the early usage of the Greek and Latin Churches may have originated the custom of observing twelve days as the Christmas holidays.

The Epiphany is said to denote Christ's manifesta-

new style, falls on the Eve of Epiphany or Twelfth-Day, and in some places, says Mr. Hone, " is still observed as the festival of the Nativity."

tion to the world in four several respects, which at first were all commemorated upon this day, namely: (1.) By his Nativity or Incarnation. (2.) By the appearance of the Star which guided the Wise Men unto Christ at his birth. (3.) By the glorious appearance that was made at his baptism. (4.) By the manifestation of his Divinity, when by his first miracle He turned the water into wine, at the marriage of Cana in Galilee.

In England the twelve days of Christmas were certainly observed as early as the time of Alfred the Great, and probably from a much earlier period. Collier, in his "Ecclesiastical History of Britain," cites a law of Alfred in which, "the twelve days after the Nativity of our Saviour are made holy days."

The Magi, or "Wise Men of the East," commemorated at the Epiphany, are supposed to have been Persians. These Magi in their own country were philosophers or priests, and besides were sometimes royal counselors, physicians, astrologers, or mathematicians. In fact they were similar to the Brahmins of India, the Philosophers among the Greeks, and the Druids among the Gauls. Zoroaster, one of their number and King of Bactria, the great reformer of the sect of the Magi, has left on record a curious prophecy relating to the future birth of a Saviour, and its announcement by a Star, which seems to agree in a remarkable manner with that of Balaam : " There shall come a Star out of Jacob, and a Sceptre shall rise out of Israel." Says Abul Pharajius, speaking of Zoroaster, —

"He taught the Persians the manifestation of the Lord Christ, commanding that they should bring him gifts ; and revealed to them that it would happen in the latter time that a virgin would conceive without contact with a man, and that when her child was born, a star would appear and shine by day, in the midst of which would be seen the figure of a virgin. 'But you, my children, will see its rising before all the nations. When, therefore, ye shall behold it, go whither the star shall guide ye and adore the child, and offer up to him your gifts, seeing that he is the Word, which has created the Heavens.'"

Blunt says : —

"Some authors have suggested, and it seems not improbable, that the '*Star*' which appeared to the Wise Men in the East might be that glorious light which shone upon the Shepherds of Bethlehem, when the angels came to give them the glad tidings of our Saviour's birth. According to an ancient commentary on St. Matthew, this Star, on its first appearance to the Magi, had the form of a radiant child bearing a sceptre or cross ; and in some early Italian frescoes, it is so depicted."

The Wise Men who came to Jerusalem in the days of Herod, are traditionally believed to have been three in number, and of the rank of kings or princes. The Venerable Bede, in the seventh century, was the first writer in England who gave a description of them, which he is supposed to have taken from some earlier account. According to Bede, —

"Melchior was old, with gray hair and long beard, and offered gold to our Saviour in acknowledgment of his sovereignty ; Jaspar was young, without any beard, and offered frankincense in recognition of the Divinity ; and Balthasar was of a dark complexion as a Moor, with a large spreading beard, and offered myrrh to our Saviour's humanity."

The tradition is that they were baptized by St. Thomas, and afterwards themselves preached the gospel.   In the fourth century their bodies were said to have been discovered by the Empress Helena, and taken to Constantinople; from thence to Milan; and when that city was taken by the Emperor Frederick in 1164, he gave these relics to Reinaldus, Archbishop of Cologne, whence they are commonly called " The Three Kings of Cologne."

In England, a striking memorial of the offerings of the Magi is kept up by the sovereigns, who make an oblation of gold, frankincense, and myrrh, at the Altar of the Chapel Royal in the Palace of St. James, on this festival.

Le Neve's manuscript, called " The Royal Book," containing the method of keeping festivals at court in the reign of Henry the Seventh, prescribes " That on Twelfth-day the King must go crowned in his royal robes, kirtle, surcoat, his furred hood about his neck, his mantle with a long train, and his cutlas before him; his armills upon his arms, of gold set full of rich stones ; and no temporal man to touch it, but the King himself; and the squire for the body must bring it to the King in a fair kerchief, and the King must put them on himself ; and he must have his sceptre in his right hand,

and the ball with the cross in his left hand, and the crown upon his head. And he must offer that day, gold, myrrh, and cense; then must the dean of the chapel send unto the Archbishop of Canterbury by clerk or priest, the King's offering that day; and then must the Archbishop give the next benefice that falleth in his gift to the same messenger."

"A century ago," says Mr. Chambers, "the king, preceded by heralds, pursuivants, and the Knights of the Garter, Thistle, and Bath, in the collars of their respective orders, went to the Royal Chapel of St. James' and offered gold, myrrh, and frankincense, in imitation of the Eastern Magi's offering to our Saviour. Since the illness of George III., the procession, and even the personal appearance of the monarch, have been discontinued. Two gentlemen from the Lord Chamberlain's office now appear instead, attended by a box ornamented at top with a spangled star from which they take the gold, frankincense, and myrrh, and place them on an alms-dish held forth by the officiating priest."

The story of the Three Kings of Cologne forms the subject of many of the early " mysteries," formerly so popular. There are, indeed, said to have been representations of the Magi in the French churches as early as the fifth century, and there are French mysteries relating to them in the eleventh century, and also a Latin one, wherein Virgil (who appears to have usually taken a conspicuous part in mediæval pageantry, and was supposed to have been a magician), accompanies the kings on their journey, and at the end of the adoration joins them very devoutly in the "bene-dicamus."

" The Feast of the Three Kings " was first performed by the Monks of the Mendicant Order, who studied the arts of popular entertainment in Milan, in 1366. " On the Feast of Epiphany," says the Italian chronicler, Gualvanei de la Flamma, "the first feast of the three kings was celebrated at Milan by the convent of the friars' Preachers. The three kings appeared crowned, on three great horses, richly habited, surrounded by pages, body-guards, and an innumerable retinue. A golden star was exhibited in the sky, going before them. They proceeded to the pillars of St. Lawrence, where king Herod was represented with his scribes and wise men. The three kings ask Herod where Christ should be born ; and his wise men, having consulted their books, answer him, at Bethlehem. On which, the three kings with their golden crowns, having in their hands golden cups filled with frankincense, myrrh, and gold, the star still going before, marched to the church of St. Eustor-gius, with all their attendants ; preceded by trumpets, and horns, apes, baboons, and a great variety of animals. In the church, on one side of the high altar, there was a manger with an ox and an ass, and in it the infant Christ in the arms of his mother. Here the three kings offer their gifts, etc. The concourse of the peo-ple, of knights, ladies, and ecclesiastics, was such as never before was beheld."

Du Cange gives a very similar account of the custom which was once prevalent in France : At the Feast of the Star, that is, the Epiphany, " Three of the principal Canons rode in procession to church with crowns upon their heads, dressed in royal robes, and carrying in their hands golden boxes, containing the offerings of gold, frankincense, and myrrh. A gilt star, raised by some mechanical contrivance, was drawn before them. There was a band of music, and they had many attendants disguised as baboons, apes, and other wild animals."

The Adoration of the Magi was a favorite subject in our early English mysteries. In " Dives and Pauper," 1496, we read : " For to represente in playnge at Crystmasse Herodes and the Thre Kynges and other processes of the gospelles both than and at Ester, and at other times also, it is befull and comendable."

These mysteries were suppressed early in the time of James the First; but the Adoration of the Magi was afterwards introduced as a puppet show at Bartholomew Fair, as late as the time of Queen Anne.

This representation of the Adoration of the Magi has given place in more modern times, at least in France and England, to the still popular game of drawing for king and queen of Twelfth-Night. This custom has generally been supposed to be in honor of the Three Kings of Cologne; although Mr. Soane thinks that in all probability it owes its origin to a

Greek and Roman custom of casting lots at their banquets for who should be the "*Rex Convivii*," or as Horace calls him, the "*Arbiter Bibendi*."[1] However, this custom, according to Strutt, "was a common Christmas gambol in both of the English universities, previous to the beginning of the last century."

An old calendar says: "On the 5th of January — the Vigil of the Epiphany — the Kings of the Bean are created, and on the 6th the feast of the Kings shall be held, and also of the Queen, and let the banqueting be continued for many days."

The usage now in regard to this game — particularly in France and England — is to place a bean and pea (or ring) in a Twelfth-cake, which, being divided, is distributed, and the persons finding the bean and pea, are the King and Queen of Twelfth-Night.

Two hundred years ago the ingredients of the bean-cake were flour, honey, ginger, and pepper. "But it would not compete," says Mr. Sandys, "with that beautiful, frosted, festooned, bedizened, and ornamented piece of confectionery, now called, *par eminence*, 'Twelfth-cake,' with its splendid waxen or plaster-of-paris kings and queens, the delight and admiration of school-boys and girls."

In some parts of France the Bean-King is elected by another process. A child is placed under a table

---

[1] "After the rose and ivy wreaths and perfumes and ointments had been distributed, the chairman or king of the feast was chosen by throw of dice. He who threw Venus, or the six, became king. The lowest cast was called the dog." — *The Albion.*

where he can see nothing; and the master of the feast, holding up a piece of cake, demands whose portion it is to be. The child replies according to his own fancy, and this game continues till the piece which contains the bean has been allotted. A whole court is thus formed, the *fool* not being forgotten, and every time either of these magistrates is seen to drink, the company are bound to cry out under pain of forfeit, " The King (or the Queen) drinks."

In London, it is or was the custom for the Lord Mayor to give a Twefth-Night Party at the Mansion House. The King and Queen of the Bean were chosen by lot, and were surrounded not by " baboons, apes, and other wild animals," but by highly respectable ladies and gentlemen who wore on their sleeves pictorial representations of grotesque Twelfth-Night Characters,[1] which they were expected to sustain, modern notions not permitting a nearer approach to mediæval Christmas Mummery.

In short, the " Feast of the Star," known in France as " Fête des Rois;" in the Low Countries as " Driekoningendag" (The Day of the Three Kings); and throughout Germany as the " Tag der Heiligen dree

[1] Britton, in his Autobiography, tells us he "suggested and wrote a series of Twelfth-Night Characters to be printed on cards, placed in a bag, and drawn out at parties on the memorable and merry evenings of that ancient festival. They were sold in small packets to pastry-cooks, and led the way to a custom which annually grew to an extensive trade. For the second year my pen and ink characters were accompanied by prints of the different personages by Cruikshank (father of the inimitable George), all of a comic or ludicrous kind."

Konige " [" Feast of the Three Holy Kings "], has been generally observed from a very early period as a popular and domestic holiday.

" Cologne, of course, celebrates with great pomp and noise and public festivity, the day of the venerated Kings whose relics she guards. . . . . Everywhere it is the children's favorite holiday. In many places fairs are held with booths full of toys, trinkets, and confectionary ; while masked or fantastically decorated processions roam about the streets headed by three crowned children. Even in sober, methodical, commercial Lutheran Hamburg, business is suspended. . . . . Friendly presents are given and all the children made happy by their holiday wealth as well as by their holiday frolicks.   The morning opens with merry chimes from the church towers, the streets are vocal all day with the chants and carols of chorister-boys, in houses, public and private, rises the smell of the feast, mixed with the perfumes of flowers and of Rhein wein. . . . . On that sixth of January night, in that far northern city swept by keen blasts from the North Sea, it must be a wild night, indeed, which can prevent the streets from being vocal with music and song. . . . . Throughout the Netherlands, whether Belgian or Batavian, in both branches of the separated but kindred people, Flemish and Low Dutch, this same festival ' de Drinckoningenfeest ' is observed by all classes.   It is kept more as a social holiday by the Hollanders, and in Flanders with more of the external ceremonial of Cologne ; but in both, the general custom of election by lot prevails, and in both there is a display and consumption of cakes and ' cookies ' of all sorts, which would put Herrick's ' mighty cakes ' out of countenance."

In our own metropolis, we have had a recent (1858) example of its festive influence.   The Century Club of New York, having built a new and spacious clubhouse, selected Twelfth-Night as the most appropriate season for its inauguration.[1] Nothing of antique splendor seems to have been wanting on the occasion. The whole building, like the baronial hall of the olden time, was devoted to the festival. At "half-past ten o'clock the company had assembled, when the Herald, richly clothed in an official costume, approached the President and handed him a baton of office, and then preceded him to the foot of the throne, making way among the crowd as he passed. The President announced that an election for King and Queen of Twelfth-Night would take place, according to time-honored usage, and he directed the Herald to make proclamation to that effect, which duty that officer performed with a flourish of his trumpet, calling upon the assembly to attend to this august ceremony. The election was held in keeping with ancient form, the symbols of the royal office being deposited in a Twelfth-Night cake, which was cut up and handed around on massive silver salvers. During this ceremony and the proceeding of election, the whole court advanced in procession, an imposing retinue of characteristic personages, with pages, in white satin, bearing the two crowns on splendid red cushions, whilst choristers in antique garbs, chanted alternately, the Boar's Head Hymn to an ancient tune, supported in chorus by numerous voices. and with a most effective orchestra."

These Christmas Mummeries, in spite of certain in-

[1] See *Twelfth-Night at the Century Club, New York*, 1858. [Appleton & Co.]

novations and irregularities gave great satisfaction to
the numerous and distinguished company assembled.
The "Bringing in of the Boar's Head" ought to have
been *at* and not *before* the supper which followed the
installation ceremonies of the King and Queen, whilst
for a coronation anthem nothing could have been more
appropriate than Herrick's Twelfth-Night Song :[1]—

> "Now, now the mirth comes,
>   With the cake full of plums,
>   Where Bean 's the King of the sports here ;
>   Besides, we must know,
>   The Pea also
>   Must revel as Queen in the court here.
>
> " Begin then to choose,
>   This night as you use,
>   Who shall, for the present delight here,
>   Be a King by the lot,
>   And who shall not
>   Be Twelfth-Day Queen for the night here.
>
> "Which known, let us make
>   Joy-sops with the cake ;
>   And let not a man then be seen here,
>   Who, unurged, will not drink,
>   To the base from the brink,
>   A health to the king and the queen here.
>
> "Next crown the bowl full
>   With gentle lamb's wool ;
>   Add sugar, nutmeg, and ginger,

---

[1] This carol has been set to music by Novello.

With store of ale too ;
And thus must ye do
   To make the wassail a swinger.

"Give then to the King
  And Queen wassailing ;
   And though with ale ye be wet here,
Yet part ye from hence,
As free from óffense,
   As when ye innocent met here."

CHAPTER XII.

SHROVE-TIDE ; OR CARNIVAL.

H E Festival of the Purification [Feb. 2d], commonly called Candlemas Day,[1] has from very early times been considered the extreme limit of the Christmas Holidays.

Now the evergreens must be removed : —

Down with the rosemary and bays,
Down with the mistletoe ;
. . . .
That so the superstitious find
Not one least branch left
there behind ;

---

[1] The custom of carrying candles in procession on Candlemas Day, was especially enjoined by Henry VIII. The King in royal proclamation (1539) says :

For look, how many leaves there be
Neglected there, maids, trust to me
So many goblins you shall see.

Now the Lord of Misrule, dismounting from his hobby-horse, must lay aside his baton of authority, and like his quondam willing subjects henceforth submit himself to the rule of Right Reason. Now vacations have come to an end, and scholars must return to books and to birch, for, in the words of the old Scotch rhymes : —

Yule's come and Yule's gane
And we hae feasted weel;
Sae Jock maun to his flail again,
And Jenny to her wheel.

In days of yore, however, there was a partial revival of holiday sports and pastimes at Shrove-tide, " which among the Roman Catholics was the time appointed for *shriving or confession of sins*, and was also observed as a carnival before the commencement of Lent. The former of these ceremonies, says Mr. Drake, was dispensed with at the Reformation; but the rites attending the latter were for a time supported with a rival spirit of hilarity. The Monday and Tuesday succeeding Shrove-Sunday, called Collop Monday, and Pancake Tuesday, were peculiarly devoted to Shrove-

" On Candlemas Day, it shall be declared that the bearing of candles is done in memory of Christ, the spiritual light whom Simeon did prophesy, as it is read in the Church that day."

tide amusements, the first having been, in papal times, the period at which they took leave of flesh, or slices of meat, termed *collops*, in the north, which had been preserved through the winter by salting and drying, and the second was a relic of the feast preceding Lent; eggs and collops therefore on the Monday, and pancakes, as a delicacy, on the Tuesday, were duly if not religiously served up."

"Shrove or Pancake Tuesday, is still called in the North of England, Fastens, or Fasterns' E'en, as preceding Ash Wednesday, the first day of Lent; and the turning of these cakes is yet observed as a feat of . dexterity and skill."

Taylor, the Water Poet, in his "Jack-a-Lent" works, 1630, gives the following curious account of the Shrove-Tuesday observances of his time : —

"Shrove-Tuesday at whose entrance in the morning all the whole kingdom is in quiet, but by that time the clock strikes eleven, which (by the help of a knavish sexton) is commonly before nine, then there is a bell rung, cal'd the Pancake-bell, the sound whereof makes thousands of people distracted, and forgetfull either of manners or humanitie ; then there is a thing cald wheaten flowre, which the cookes doe mingle with water, egges, spice, and other tragicall, magicall inchantments, and then they put it by little into a frying-pan of boyling suet, where it makes a confused dismall hissing (like the Learnean snakes in the reeds of Acheron, Stix or Phlegethon) untill, at last, by the skill of the cooke, it is transferred into the form of a Flap-jack, cal'd a Pancake, which ominous incantation the ignorant people doe devoure very greedily."

This Pancake-bell, which in ancient times called the

faithful to confession, still continues in some places to summon people to the more cheerful occupation above described.

According to the " Book of Days," this custom is still observed with great solemnity at the Westminster School : —

"At 11 o'clock, A. M., a verger of the Abbey, in his gown, bearing a silver mace, emerges from the college kitchen, followed by the cook of the school, in his white apron, jacket, and cap, and carrying a pancake. On arriving at the school-room door, he announces himself ' The Cook ; ' and having entered the school-room, he advances to the bar which separates the upper school from the lower one, twirls the pancake in the pan, and then tosses it over the bar into the upper school, among a crowd of boys who scramble for the pancake ; and he who gets it unbroken, and carries it to the Deanery, demands the honorarium of a guinea (sometimes two guineas) from the Abbey funds ; though the custom is not mentioned in the Abbey Statutes. The cook also receives two guineas for his performance."

The custom of cock-throwing was a diversion peculiar to Shrove-tide, and is said to have originated in the barbarous yet less savage amusement of cock-fighting. According to Fitzstephen, who wrote in the reign of Henry II., " Every year on Shrove-Tuesday, that we may begin with children's sports, seeing we all have been children, the school-boys do bring cocks of the game to their master, and all the forenoon they delight themselves in cock-fighting."

At what period this degenerated into cock-throwing cannot now be ascertained. The first effective blow directed against the sport appears to have been given

by Hogarth, who in one of his prints called " The Four
Stages of Cruelty," has represented among other puerile
diversions, a group of boys throwing at a cock.

Hilman gives the following amusing account of a
somewhat similar Shrove-tide custom known as thresh-
ing the fat hen : " The hen," says he, " is hung at a fellow's back, who has also some horse-bells about him;
the rest of the fellows are blinded, and have boughs in
their hands with which they chase this fellow and his
hen about some large court or small enclosure. The
fellow with his hen and bells shifting as well as he can,
they follow the sound, and sometimes hit him and his
hen ; and at other times if he can get behind one of
them, they thresh one another well favour'dly, but the
jest is, the maids are to blind the fellows, which they
do with their aprons, and the cunning baggages will
endear their sweet-hearts with a peeping hole, whilst
the others look out as sharp to hinder it. After this
the hen is boiled with bacon, and store of pancakes
and flitters are made. She that is noted for lying in
bed long, or any other miscarriage, hath the first pancake presented to her which most commonly falls to
the dogs' share at last, for no one will own it their
due."

" The evening of Shrove-Tuesday," says Mr. Drake,
" was usually appropriated, as well in the country as in
the town, to the exhibition of dramatic pieces. Not
only at Court, where Jonson was occasionally employed
to write Masques on this night, but at both the univer-

sities, in the provincial schools, and in the halls of the gentry and nobility were these the amusements of Shrove-tide, during the days of Elizabeth and James."[1] At Shrove-tide the Inns of Court had what they called Post Revels, coming as Dugdale says, "at the latter end of Christmas," and among the Masques and pageants described in the preceding pages, none could have been more interesting than those of the years 1612–1613.

"Seldom," says Mr. Jeaffreson, "had the Thames presented a more picturesque and exhilarating spectacle than it did on the evening of February 20, 1612, when the gentlemen masquers of Gray's Inn and the Temple, entered the king's royal barge at Winchester House, at seven o'clock, and made the voyage to Whitehall, attended by hundreds of barges and boats, each vessel being so brilliantly illuminated that the lights reflected upon the ripples of the river seemed to be countless. As though the hum and huzzas of the vast multitude on the water were insufficient to announce the approach of the dazzling pageant, guns marked the progress of the revellers, and as they drew near the palace, all the attendant bands of musicians played the same stirring tune with uniform time. It is on record that the king received the amateur actors with an excess of condescension, and was delighted with the masque which Master Beaumont of the Inner Temple, and his friend Master Fletcher, had written and dedicated 'to the worthy Sir Francis Bacon, his Majesty's Solicitor General, and the grave and learned

---

[1] In a chronological series of Queen Elizabeth's payments for plays acted before her is the following entry, 18th March, 1573-4 : " To Richard Mouncaster [Mulcaster, the Grammarian] for two plays presented before her on Candlemas-day and Shrove-tuesday last, 20 marks." In the Percy Household Book, 1512, it appears that the clergy and officers of Lord Percy's Chapel, performed a play *before his lordship upon Shrove-tuesday at night.*

bench of the anciently-called houses of Grayes Inn, and the Inner
Temple, and the Inner Temple and Grayes Inn.' The Inner Temple and Gray's Inn having thus testified their loyalty and dramatic
taste; in the following year, on Shrove-Monday Night (February 15,
1613), Lincoln's Inn and the Middle Temple, with no less splendor
and *éclat*, enacted at Whitehall, a masque, written by George Chap-
man. For this entertainment, Inigo Jones designed and perfected
the theatrical decorations in a style worthy of an exhibition that
formed part of the gayeties with which the marriage of the Palsgrave
with the Princess Elizabeth was celebrated. And though the
masquers went to Whitehall by land, their progress was not less
pompous than the procession which had passed up the Thames in
the February of the preceding year. Having mustered in Chancery
Lane, at the official residence of the Master of the Rolls, the actors
and their friends delighted the town with a gallant spectacle.
Mounted on richly-caparisoned and mettlesome horses, they rode
from Fleet Street up the Strand, and by Charing Cross to Whitehall,
through a tempest of enthusiasm. Every house was illuminated,
every window was crowded with faces, on every roof men stood in
rows, from every balcony bright eyes looked down upon the gay
scene, and from basement to garret, from kennel to roof-top
throughout the long way, deafening cheers testified, whilst they
increased the delight of the multitude. Such a pageant would, even
in these sober days, rouse London from her cold propriety. Having thrown aside his academic robe, each masquer had donned a
fantastic dress of silver cloth embroidered with gold lace, gold
plate, and ostrich plumes. He wore across his breast a gold bal-
drick, round his neck a ruff of white feathers brightened with pearls
and silver lace, and on his head a coronal of snowy plumes. Before each mounted masquer rode a torch bearer, whose right hand
waved a scourge of flame, instead of a leathern thong. In a gorgeous chariot, preceded by a long train of heralds, were exhibited the
Dramatis Personæ — Honor, Plutus, Eunomia, Phemeis, Capriccio
— arrayed in their appointed costume; and it was rumored that

the golden canopy of their coach had been bought for an enormous sum. Two other triumphal cars conveyed the twelve chief musicians of the kingdom, and these masters of melody were guarded by torchbearers, marching two deep before and behind, and on either side of the glittering carriages. Preceding the musicians, rode a troop of ludicrous objects, who roused the derision of the mob, and made fat burghers laugh till tears ran down their cheeks. They were the mock masque, each resembling an ape, each wearing a fantastic dress that heightened the hideous absurdity of his monkey's visage, each riding upon an ass, or small pony, and each of them throwing shells upon the crowd by way of largess. In the front of the mock masque, forming the vanguard of the entire spectacle, rode fifty gentlemen of the Inns of Court, reigning high bred horses, and followed by their running foot-men, whose liveries added to the gorgeous magnificence of the display."

Among the favorite amusements at Shrove-tide, even so early as the time of Henry II., was the game of football. According to Fitzstephen : " After dinner, all the youth of the city goeth to play at the ball in the fields ; the scholars of every study have their balls ; the practises also of all the trades have every one their ball in their hands. The ancienter sort, the fathers and the wealthier citizens, come on horse-back, to see these youngsters contending at their sport, with whom, in a manner, they participate by motion ; stirring their own natural heat in the view of the active youth, with whose mirth and liberty they seem to communicate."

Brand says : —

" With regard to the custom of playing at foot-ball on Shrove-Tuesday, I was informed that at Alnwick Castle in Northumberland,

the waits belonging to the town came playing to the castle every
year on Shrove-Tuesday, at two o'clock, P. M., when a foot-ball was
thrown over the castle walls to the populace.   I saw this done February 5, 1788."

Billet, or Tip-cat, was also a popular game for this
day, and in some parts of the North of England it is
customary for the girls to occupy some part of the
festival by the game of battledoor and shuttlecock,
singing : —

> " Great A, little A,
>   This is Pancake Day ;
>   Toss the ball high,
>   Throw the ball low,
>   Those that come after
>   May sing heigh-ho ! "

In Sir John Sinclair's " Statistical Account of Scotland," 1795, we read : " On Shrove-Tuesday there is a
standing match at foot-ball between the married and
unmarried women, in which the former are always vic-
torious."   In the same work we read : " Every year on
Shrove-Tuesday the bachelors and married men drew
themselves up at the Cross of Scone on opposite sides.
A ball was then thrown up, and they played from
two o'clock till sunset."

This custom is supposed to have had its origin in
the days of chivalry.   An Italian, it is said, came into
this part of the country, challenging all the parishes
under a certain penalty in case of declining his chal-

lenge. All the parishes declined the challenge except Scone, which beat the foreigner, and in commemoration of this gallant action the game was instituted. Whilst the custom continued, every man in the parish, the gentry not excepted, was obliged to turn out and support the side to which he belonged, and the person who neglected to do his part on that occasion was fined.

Another singular Shrove-tide contest carried on by boys and girls in Kent, is thus described in the "Gentleman's Magazine," 1772. The custom appears to be a remnant of ancient Carnival or Shrove-tide merriment, of which but few traces are now to be found among the popular observances of the times : —

"Being on a visit on Tuesday last, in a little obscure village in this county, I found an odd kind of sport going forward ; the girls, from eightçen to five or six years old, were assembled in a crowd, and burning an uncouth effigy, which they called an Holly-boy, and which it seems they had stolen from the boys ; who, in another part of the village, were assembled together and burning what they called an Ivy-girl, which they had stolen from the girls. All this ceremony was accompanied with loud huzzas, noise, and acclamations. What it all means I cannot tell, although I inquired of several of the oldest people in the place, who could only answer that it had always been a sport at this season of the year."

The holly and the ivy being Christmas evergreens, the ceremony described may perhaps have been a facetious way of signifying that the Christmas holidays were at last come to an end.

The following quaint old carol of the time of Henry VI. seems to have reference to some such custom as that just described : —

NAY, IVY, NAY!

"Nay, Ivy, nay, it shall not be, I wis,
Let Holly have the mastery, as the manner is.
　　Holly standeth in the hall fair to behold,
　　Ivy stands without the door ; she is full sore a cold.
　　　　　　　　Nay, Ivy, nay, etc.

"Holly and his merry men, they dance now and they sing ;
Ivy and her maidens, they weep, and their hands wring.
　　　　　　　　Nay, Ivy, nay, etc.

"Ivy hath a lybe,[1] she caught it with the cold,
So may they all have, that do with Ivy hold.
　　　　　　　　Nay, Ivy, nay, etc.

"Holly he hath berries, as red as any rose,
The foresters, the hunters, keep them from the does.
　　　　　　　　Nay, Ivy, nay, etc.

"Ivy she hath berries, as black as any sloe,
There come the owls and eat them as they go.
　　　　　　　　Nay, Ivy, nay, etc.

"Holly he hath birds, a full fair flock,
The nightingale, the poppinjay, the gentle laverock.
　　　　　　　　Nay, Ivy, nay, etc.

---

[1] The word is not explained by any glossary.

" Good Ivy say to us, what birds hast thou ?
None but the owlet that cries, ' How ! How ! '
Nay, Ivy, nay," etc.

The following from Mr. Wright's MS. seems also to
have reference to this sylvan warfare, which appears to
have been conducted with rustic courtesy, and in the
true spirit of chivalry : —

" Holly and Ivy made a great party,
Who should have the mastery
In lands where they go.

" Then spake Holly, ' I am fierce and jolly,
I will have the mastery
In lands where we go.'

" Then spake Ivy, ' I am loud and proud,
And I will have the mastery
In lands where we go.'

" Then spake Holly, and bent him down on his knee,
' I pray thee, gentle Ivy, essay me no villainy,
In lands where we go.' "

CHAPTER XIII.

THE term Easter is derived, as some suppose, from the Saxon "Oster," to rise; this being the day of Christ's rising from the dead. Others, however, maintain that this Queen of Christian festivals, takes its name from Eoster or Easter, a Saxon goddess whose religious rites were celebrated in the beginning of Spring.

Soane suggests that the Saxon *Easter* or *Eoster*, the Greek Ἀστήρ, the

English *Star*, and the Hebrew *Ashtaroth*, have all come from the same long-forgotten original, perhaps Phœnician, word signifying " Fire."

It was anciently the custom in England to put out all the fires and relight them on Easter-Even, from consecrated flints preserved in churches specially for that purpose. The popular belief was that holy fire, obtained in this manner, would prevent the effect of storms, etc. Fosbrooke, quoting Rupert, says, " The flint signified Christ, and the fire the Holy Ghost."

The custom of putting out the fire in the hall also at this season, appears to have been connected with this ecclesiastical observance. The "Festival" (1511), referring to this domestic usage, says : —

" This day (Easter) is called, in many places, Goddes Sondaye ; ye know well that it is the maner at this daye to do the fyre out of the hall, and the black Wynter brandes, and all thynges that is foule with fume and smoke shall be done awaye, and there the fyre was, shall be gayly arayed with fayre flowres, and strewed with grene rysshes all aboute."

Dr. Drake in his work, " Shakespeare and his Times," says that, " Easter was formerly a season of great social festivities; " and also that, " it was customary for the common people — even as they do still in Ireland — to rise early on Easter morning to see the sun dance." Metaphorically considered, the thought may be termed both just and beautiful ; for as " the earth and her valleys standing thick with corn " are said to "laugh and sing," so, on account of the glory of the Resurrection, the sun may be said to "dance" for joy — the natural rising of the sun being, as it were, typical of the rising of the "Sun of Righteousness" from the darkness of the grave. The earth also, awaking at this season from its death-like wintry slumber, seems to make an appropriate response to this celestial demonstration of joy by its own most beautiful Easter offering of Spring flowers.

This idea has been happily expressed by Paulinus, Bishop of Nola (431) : —

> "Sing praises to your God, ye youths, and pay your holy vows,
>   The floor with many flowers strew, the threshold bind with
>   boughs ;
> Let Winter breathe a fragrance forth, like as the purple Spring ;
> Let the young year, before the time, its floral treasures bring
> And Nature yield, to this Great Day, herself an offering."

In addition to the use of flowers at Easter, our pious forefathers symbolized the cardinal doctrine of the Christian Faith, even in their holiday sports and pastimes.

One of the most curious of these popular observances is that of "lifting" or "heaving," which is undoubtedly a vulgar representation of the Resurrection. The kiss, which forms an essential part of the usage, is still the appropriate Easter salutation in the Greek Church.[1]

[1] " All the inhabitants in festival array, were hurrying along to pay their visits and receive their congratulations, every one as he met his friend, saluted him with a kiss on each side of his face, and repeated the words Χριστος ἀνέστη — "Christ is risen." — *Easter in the Greek Church.*

Such recreations may seem to us childish, if not profane, but in other days they may have been very edi-
fying to simple-minded folk.

The ceremony has been thus described : —

"On Easter-Monday the men lift the women ; and on Easter-
Tuesday the women lift, or heave, the men. The process is performed by two lusty men, or women, joining their hands across each
other's wrists ; then, making the person to be heaved, sit down on
their arms, they lift him up aloft three times, and often carry him
several yards along a street. At the end of the ceremony the person lifted is duly kissed by the lifters, and a forfeit claimed. Some
times, instead of crossed hands, a chair or bed is used."

Mr. Ellis inserts in his edition of Brand's " Popular
Antiquities " a letter from Mr. Thomas Loggan, of
Basinghall Street, London, in which he says : —

"I was sitting alone last Easter-Tuesday at breakfast, at the
Talbot Inn, Shrewsbury, when I was surprised by the entrance of
all the female servants of the house handing in an arm-chair, lined
with white, and decorated with ribbons and favors of different colors.
I asked them what they wanted : their answer was, they came to
heave me ; it was the custom of the place on that morning, and they
hoped I would take a seat in their chair. It was impossible not to
comply with a request very modestly made, and by a set of nymphs
in their best apparel, and several of them under twenty. I wished
to see all the ceremony, and seated myself accordingly. The group
then lifted me from the ground, turned the chair about, and I had
the felicity of a salute from each. I told them I supposed there was
a fee on the occasion, and was answered in the affirmative, and having satisfied the damsels in this respect, they withdrew to heave
others. At this time I had never heard of such a custom ; but on

inquiry I found that on Easter-Monday, between nine and twelve, the men heave the women, in the same manner as on the Tuesday, between the same hours, the women heave the men."

This custom of "heaving" is probably of Oriental origin and may have been brought from the East by the Crusaders. In the time of the Plantagenets it was a courtly ceremony, differing from its "survival" in degree rather than in principle, for we find from a roll in the custody of the Keeper of the Records in the Tower of London, that certain ladies and maids of honor received payment for taking King Edward I. in his bed at Easter : —

"To the ladies of the Queen's chamber 15th of May; seven ladies and damsels of the Queen, because they took (or lifted) the King in his bed, on the morrow of Easter, and made him pay fine for the peace of the King, which he made of his gift by the hand of Hugh de Cerr (or Kerr), Esq., to the Lady of Weston, £14."

Perhaps the nursery pastime of "making a chair," still in vogue among children, is a relic of this ancient custom.

The game of hand-ball, however, another of the Easter sports, appears to have had a very different fortune, and to have developed itself into those most manly of athletic sports, cricket and base-ball.

In ancient times, say the Ritualists Belethus and Durandus —

" The bishops and archbishops on the Continent used to recreate themselves in the game of hand-ball with their inferior clergy ; and in

England, also, the game appears to have been made a part of the regular Church service at Chester. Bishops and deans took the ball into the Cathedral, and at the commencement of the antiphon, began to dance, throwing the ball to the choristers, who handed it to each other during the time of the dancing and antiphon."

Dancing, during some thousands of years was a religious ceremony. In the Temples of Jerusalem, Samaria, and Alexandria, a stage for these exercises was erected in one part, thence called the choir, the name of which has been preserved in our churches, and the custom too, it seems, till within a few centuries. Cardinal Ximenes revived in his time the practice of Mosarabic Masses in the Cathedral of Toledo, when the people danced, both in the choir and in the nave, with great decorum and devotion.

In England, corporate bodies used to join with their burgesses and young people in their Easter games. Such was once the custom, says Mr. Brand, at Newcastle, at the Feasts of Easter and Whitsuntide, when the mayor, aldermen, and sheriff, accompanied by great numbers of the burgesses, used to go yearly at these seasons to the Forth or little mall of the town, with mace, sword, and cap of maintenance carried before them, and not only countenance, but frequently join in, the diversions of hand-ball, dancing, etc. There was also in the ancient city of Chester a similar custom, when at the great Festival of Easter, " The mayor and corporation, with the twenty guilds established in Chester, with their wardens at their heads, set forth in all their pageantry to the Rood-eye (an open meadow by the river side), to play at foot-ball. The mayor with his mace, sword, and cap of maintenance, stood before the Cross, whilst the guild of shoemakers, to whom the right had belonged from time immemorial, presented him with the ball of the value of ' three and four-pence or above,' and all set to work right merrily." But as too often falls out in this game, " great strife did arise among the younge persons of the same cittie," and hence, in the time of Henry VIII., this piece of homage to the mayor was converted into a present from the shoe-makers to the drapers, of six gleaves or hand-darts of silver, to be given for the best foot-race ; whilst the saddlers, who went in procession on horseback, attired in all their bravery, each carrying a spear with a wooden ball, decorated with flowers and arms, ex-changed their offering for a silver bell, which should be a " reward for that horse which with speedy run-ninge should run before all others." These silver bells were in the seventeenth century converted into cups, or other pieces of plate, which still continue to be the " trophies of victory " at horse-races.

But the ordinary prize at games of ball during Eas-ter, was the Tansy-cake : —

> " At stool-ball, Lucia, let us play
> For sugar cakes and wine ;
> Or for a tansy let us play,
> The loss be thine or mine.

"If thou, my dear, a winner be,
   At trundling of the ball,
The wager thou shalt have and me,
   And my misfortunes all."

These cakes were made of flour, butter, sugar, sherry, cream, and tansies; whence they derived the name of "tansays," or "tansy-cakes." The tansy having reference, says Selden, to the *bitter herbs* used by the Jews at the Passover, though at the same time, " 'twas always the fashion for a man to have a gammon of bacon to show himself to be no Jew." The Jews themselves, however, says Brady, in his "Clavis Calendaria," "long since contrived to diminish the bitter flavor of the tansy, by making it into a pickle for their Paschal Lamb, from whence we borrowed the custom of taking mint and sugar as a general sauce for that description of food."

Another custom which prevailed in the olden time, and which is still kept up both in England and Ireland, and even in this country, is that of presenting children with eggs, stained with various colors in boiling, and curiously ornamented with devices and mottoes; they are termed "paste," or more properly "Pasche Eggs." In the Greek Church likewise, says Brady, "*Eggs* still continue to form a part of the ceremonies of the day; and *there* also, presents of eggs, from one individual to another, are considered as pious attentions." This observance appears to have arisen from a belief that eggs were an emblem of the Resurrection. On this custom Mr. Brand has well observed that —

> "The ancient Egyptians, if the resurrection of the body had been a tenet of their faith, would perhaps have thought an egg no improper hieroglyphical representation of it. The exclusion of a living creature by incubation, after the vital principle has lain so long dormant or extinct, is a process so truly marvelous, that if it could be disbelieved, would be thought by some a thing as incredible, as that the Author of Life should be able to reanimate the dead."

In the "Ritual" of Pope Paul V., which was composed for the use of the British Isles, there is this prayer for the consecration of eggs : —

> "Bless, O Lord, we beseech thee, this thy creature of eggs, that it may become a wholesome sustenance to thy faithful servants, eating it in thankfulness to thee, on account of the Resurrection of our Lord."

In Lancashire and Cheshire, children still go round the village and beg eggs for the Easter dinner, accompanying their solicitation by a short song, the burden of which is addressed to the farmer's dame, asking for "an egg, bacon, cheese, or an apple, or any good thing that will make us merry ; " and ending with, "And I pray you good dame an Easter egg."

The observance in Lancashire of " Pace-egging," as it is there called, is a custom limited to the week preceding Easter Day, commencing on the Monday and finishing on the Thursday before Easter Day.

" Young men in groups, varying in number from three to twenty, dressed in various fantastic garbs, and wearing masks, some of the groups accompanied by a player or two on the violin, go from house to house singing, dancing, and capering. At most places they are liberally treated with wine, punch, or ale, dealt out to them by the host or hostess."

The origin of this custom of collecting " Pasche eggs," may have been the resumption on the part of our forefathers of eggs and of animal food at Easter, on the termination of Lent. It seems, moreover, that at this season extreme caution was to be used in partaking of food of all kinds, and nothing was to be eaten which had not been previously blessed, or had not at least the sign of the Cross made over it ; for the faithful were thought just then to be particularly subject to the attacks of evil spirits. Durandus gives a lamentable instance of the fatal consequences arising from a neglect of this precaution, and of which he was himself an eye-witness : " Two devils got possession of a young girl, and tormented her for three years," a miracle which, says Mr. Soane, " is often renewed in our own days, but with this especial difference, that when the devil now possesses a woman, he does not torment herself but others." " However, on this occasion, a cunning exorcist drove the fiends out at last, having previously made them confess that they had been lying perdu in a melon, which the girl had incautiously eaten without first making the sign of the Cross."

There has been a revival in modern times, even in this cóuntry, of the old Easter custom of "pace-egging." We refer to the usage of presenting one's friends on the morning of Easter Day, with a basket of pace-eggs. A dozen of these, of various colors, with mottoes and emblematic devices, artistically arranged in a fancy basket, make indeed a very appropriate Easter decoration for the drawing-room table, quietly greeting us with that most ancient of Easter salutations (still retained in the Greek Church),[1] "Christ is risen ! "[2]

[1] " No meetings take place of any kind without repeating the expressions of peace and joy. *Christos voscress !* Christ is risen ! To which the answer is always the same, *Vo istiney voscress !* He is risen indeed ! On Easter Monday begins the presentation of the paschal eggs : lovers to their mistresses, relatives to each other, servants to their masters, all bring ornamented eggs. Every offering, at this season, is called a paschal egg. The meanest pauper in the street, presenting an egg, and repeating the words *Christos voscress,* may demand a salute, even of the Empress." — *Dr. Clarke's Travels (Moscow).*

[2] For curious particulars in regard to the Easter "Sepulchre Show," see Appendix, p. 243.

CHAPTER XIV.

A N inquiry into the festivities of the Easter Holidays brings us to the consideration of those parochial processionings which in England distinguishes the season known in the Calendar as the Rogation Days. Rogation Sunday is the fifth Sunday after Easter, so called from the Latin *rogare*, ' to ask'; the Gospel for the Day, "teaching us how to ask of God so as we may obtain."

The ancient custom of Perambulating or " Beating

the Bounds" of parishes, in Rogation Week, had, it is said, a twofold object. It was designed to supplicate the divine blessing on the fruits of the earth, and to preserve in all classes of the community a correct knowledge of, and due respect for, the bounds of parochial and individual property.

> " That every man might keep his own possessions,
> Our fathers used in reverent processions,
> (With zealous prayers, and with praisefull cheere),
> To walk the parish. limits once a year." —
>
> *Wither,* 1635.

It appears that these Rogation ceremonies originated in the fifth century, in an age, says Dean Stanley, —

" Gloomy with disaster and superstition, when heathenism was still struggling with Christianity ; when Christianity was disfigured by fierce conflicts within the Church ; when the Roman Empire was tottering to its ruin ; when the last great luminary of the Church — Augustine — had just passed away, amidst the forebodings of universal destruction. The general disorder of the time was aggravated by an unusual train of calamities. Besides the ruin of society attendant on the invasion of the barbarians, there came a succession of droughts, pestilences, and earthquakes, which seemed to keep pace with the throes of the moral world. Of all these horrors, France was the centre. On one of these occasions, when the people had been hoping that with the Easter festival, some respite would come, a sudden earthquake shook the church at Vienne, on the Rhone. It was on Easter Eve ; the congregation rushed out ; the Bishop of the city (Mamertus) was left alone before the altar. On that terrible night he formed a resolution of inventing a new form, as he hoped, of drawing down the mercy of God. He determined that in the three days before Ascension Day, there should be a long procession to the nearest churches in the neighborhood. For four hundred years there were no prayers of this special kind in the Christian Church. The traveller who passes that beautiful old city (Vienne), on his way through France, may treasure up as he hurries by, the thought that along the banks of that rushing river, and from height to height of those encircling hills, were first heard the sounds of the Litany which are now so familiar. It was under a like pressure of calamities that the Litany first became part of our services."

It is the earliest portion of the " Book of Common Prayer " in its present English form.

It is not easy to say when or how these " Rogations " became mixed up with the parochial perambulations, but there cannot be the least doubt that the latter have been handed down from the times of the Romans. It is said to be only a Christian form of the *Terminalia*, established by Numa Pompilius in honor of the God Terminus, the guardian of fields and landmarks, and maintainer of peace amongst mankind.

Before the Reformation, parochial perambulations were conducted with great state and ceremony. The lord of the manor, with a large banner, priests in surplices and with crosses, and other persons with handbells and staves, followed by most of the parishioners, walked in procession round the parish, stopping at crosses, forming crosses on the ground, saying or singing gospels to the corn, and allowing drinkings and good cheer.

" In 1554," says Strype, " the priests of Queen Mary's chapel, made public processions. All the three days there went her chapel about the fields : the first to St. Giles', and there sung Mass : the next day, being Tuesday, to St. Martin's-in-the-Fields ; and there a sermon was preached, and Mass sung ; and the company drank there : the third day to Westminster, where a sermon was made, and then Mass and good cheer made ; and after about the park, and so to St. James's Court.

" The same Rogation Week, went out of the Tower on procession priests and clerks, and the Lieutenant, with all his waiters and the axe of the Tower borne in procession ; the waits [1] attended. There joined in this procession the inhabitants also of St. Catharine's, Radcliff, Limehouse, Poplar, Stratford, Bow, Shoreditch, and all those that belonged to the Tower, with their Halberts. They went about the fields of St. Catherine's and the Liberties.

" On the following Thursday, being Holy Thursday, or Ascension-Day, at the Court of St. James's, with heralds and sergeants of arms, and four Bishops, mitred, and Bishop Bonner, besides his mitre, wore a pair of slippers of silver and gold, and a pair of rich gloves with ouches of silver upon them, very rich."

At the Reformation, says the " Book of Days," the ceremonies and practices deemed objectionable, were considerably modified, and a homily was prepared for the occasion, and injunctions were issued by royal authority, requiring that for " the perambulations of the circuits of the parishes, the people should, once a year, at the time accustomed, with the rector, vicar, or

---

[1] The waits here mentioned were minstrels. At this time, it appears there were few towns of any size or note in England that did not support a band of waits, who wore a peculiar costume. Those of the city of London appeared on state occasions, in blue gowns with red sleeves, with silver badges suspended from silver collars.

curate, walk about the parishes as they were accus-tomed, and at their return to the church make their common prayer. And the curate, in their said com-mon perambulations, was at certain convenient places to admonish the people to give thanks to God (while beholding of his benefits) and for the increase and abundance of his fruits upon the face of the Earth, with the singing of the 103d Psalm."

In strict accordance with these directions, we find that " the judicious Hooker " — a faithful exemplar of a true English churchman — duly observed the custom of perambulations. At such times, he would, says his biographer, "honest Isaac Walton," "usually express more pleasant discourse than at other times, and would then always drop some loving and facetious observa-tions to be remembered against the next year, espe-cially by the boys and young people, still inclining them, and all his present parishioners, to meekness and mutual kindness and love; *because love thinks not evil, but covers a multitude of infirmities.*"

It seems, however, that sometimes instead of loving and facetious observations, sound floggings were ad-ministered to the boys, for the same desirable purpose of strengthening their memory.

According to the " Saturday Review " [February 15, 1868] : —

"At the yearly ceremony of beating parish boundaries, it was usual to beat not only the boundaries, but the boys ; or rather, perhaps, the phrase of 'beating' has been inaccurately transferred from the boys to the boundaries." [1]

Boundaries of parishes and townships were, in many points, marked out by what are called " Gospel-trees." Herrick, that stanch maintainer of old English customs, in " Hesperides," says : —

> " Dearest, bury me
> Under that Holy Oak, or Gospel Tree ;
> Where, though thou see'st not, thou may'st
> Think upon me, when thou *yearly go'st procession.*"

In Kentish Town, London, there still stands a public-house, which bears the significant sign of the Gospel Oak, taking its name from an old oak in the neighborhood, a relic of the olden time, suggestive of the once general custom of reading a portion of the Gospel for the day under certain trees, in the parish perambulations.

In Herbert's " Country Parson," we are told : —

" The Country Parson is a lover of old customs, if they be good and harmlesse. Particularly he loves *Procession*, and maintains it, because there are contained therein four manifest advantages. First, a blessing of God for the fruits of the field. 2. Justice in the

---

[1] There is a curious old Norman record illustrative of this " beating " principle : " Duke Robert, just on the point of going to the Holy Land, made a gift to the Abbey of Preaux. His son, the future Conqueror, '*adhuc puerulus,*' was sent to lay the deed of gift on the altar. Let no one suppose that irreverent hands were laid on the person of the great Bastard, even at the age of seven years. But then and there, in the young prince's presence, three other boys had their ears solemnly boxed that they might remember all about it, "*ob causam memoriæ colaphum susceperant.*"

preservation of bounds. 3. Charitie in loving, walking, and neighbourly accompanying one another, with reconciling of differences at that time, if there be any. 4. Mercie, in relieving the poor by a liberal distribution and largess, which at that time is or ought to be used. Wherefore he exacts of all to be present at the Perambulation, and those that withdraw and sever themselves from it he mislikes, and reproves as uncharitable and unneighbourly ; and if they will not reforme, presents them."

It appears that the ecclesiastic authorities at this time insisted particularly upon the religious observances of these parochial perambulations. In the Articles of Enquiry for the Archdeaconry of Northumberland, the following occurs : " Doth your Parson or Vicar observe the Three Rogation Dayes ? " In others, for the Diocese of Chichester, 1637, is the subsequent question : —

" Doth your minister yeerely, in Rogation Weeke, for the knowing and distinguishing of the bounds of parishes, and for obtaining God's blessing upon the fruites of the ground, walke the Perambulation, and say, or sing, in English, the Gospells, Epistles, Letanie, and other devout prayers ; together with the 103rd and 104th Psalmes ? "

The necessity or determination to perambulate precisely along the old track, often occasioned curious incidents. If a canal had been cut through the boundary of a parish, it was deemed necessary that some of the parishioners should pass through the water. Where a river formed part of the boundary line, the procession either passed along it in boats, or some of

11

the party stripped and swam along it, or boys were thrown into it at customary places. If a house had been erected on the boundary line, the procession claimed the right to pass through it. A ludicrous scene, it is said, occurred in London about the beginning of the present century. As the procession of church-wardens, parish officers, etc., followed by a concourse of cads, were perambulating the parish of St. George's, Hanover Square, they came to the part of a street where a nobleman's coach was standing just across the boundary line. The carriage was empty, waiting for the owner, who was in the opposite house ; the principal church-warden, — himself a nobleman, — therefore desired the coachman to drive out of their way. " I won't," said the sturdy coachman, " my lord told me to wait here, and here I will wait till his lordship tells me to move ! " The church-warden coolly opened the carriage door, entered it, passed out through the opposite door, and was followed by the whole procession, cads, sweeps, and scavengers.

The religious part of these processions has, according to Mr. Chambers, been generally omitted in more modern times.

"The custom has, however, of late years been revived in its integrity in many parishes ; and certainly, such perambulations among the bounties of creation, afford a Christian minister a most favorable opportunity for awakening in his parishioners a due sense of gratitude towards him who maketh the sun to shine, and the rains to descend upon the earth, so that it may bring forth its fruit in due season."

These perambulations occasionally took place on Ascension Day, — celebrated springs or fountains, instead of *Gospel-trees*, sometimes serving as stations. Aubrey says : —

"In Cheshire when they went in perambulation, they did blesse the springs, i. e. they did read a Gospell at them, and did believe the water was the better." [1]

An interesting account of such a ceremony as this in what is called " The Dressing of the Wells of Tissington," is given by a correspondent of "Chambers' Book of Days " (page 596). This custom seems, from the parish record, to have originated in 1615, a year of remarkable drought, when these wells furnished to the inhabitants and their cattle for ten miles round an unfailing supply of water, an element of which the English, in their moist climate, have seldom experienced the want.

"When we drove into the village, though it was only ten o'clock, we found it already full of people from many miles round, who had assembled to celebrate the feast ; for such indeed it was, all the characteristics of a village wake being there in the shape of booths, nuts, gingerbread, and toys, to delight the young. We went immediately to the church, foreseeing the difficulty there would be in getting a seat, nor were we mistaken, for though we were accommodated, numbers were obliged to remain outside, and wait for the service peculiar to the wells. The interior of the church is orna-

---

[1] We read that once in the wilderness, in a time of drought at Beer the promised well, Israel sang this song, "Spring up, O well ; sing ye unto it." — *Num.* xxi. 17.

mented with many monuments of the Fitzherbert family, and the
service was performed in rural style by a band of violinists who did
their best to make melody. As soon as the sermon was ended, the
clergyman left the pulpit, and marched at the head of the procession that was formed, into the village. After him came the band;
then the family from the Hall, and then visitors, the rest of the
congregation following; and a halt was made at the first of the
wells, which are five in number, and which we will now attempt to
describe.

"The name of 'well' scarcely gives a proper idea of these beautiful structures; they are rather fountains, or cascades, the water
descending from above, and not rising, as in a well. Their height
varies from ten to twelve feet; and the original stone frontage is on
this day hidden by a wooden erection in the form of an arch, or
some other elegant design; over these planks a layer of plaster of
Paris is spread, and while it is wet, flowers without leaves are stuck
in it, forming a most beautiful mosaic pattern On one the large
yellow field Ranunculus was arranged in letters, and so a verse of
Scripture, or of a hymn, was recalled to the spectator's mind; on
another, a white dove was sculptured in the plaster, and set in
a groundwork of the humble violet; the daisy, which our poet
Chaucer would gaze upon for hours together, formed a diaper work
of red and white; the pale yellow primrose was set off by the rich
red of the ribes; nor were the coral berries of the holly, mountain-
ash, and yew, forgotten; these are carefully gathered and stored in
the winter to be ready for the May-day fête. It is scarcely possible
to describe the vivid coloring and beautiful effect of these favorites
of nature, arranged in wreaths and garlands and devices of every
hue. And then, the pure, sparkling water, which pours down from
the midst of them unto the rustic moss-grown stones beneath, com-
pletes the enchantment, and makes this feast of the 'well-flowering'
one of the most beautiful of all the old customs that are left in
'Merrie England.'

"The groups of visitors and country people, dressed in their holiday clothes, stood reverently round, whilst the clergyman read the first of the three psalms appointed for the day, and then gave out one of Bishop Heber's beautiful hymns, in which all joined with heart and voice.

" When this was all over, all moved forwards to the next well, where the next psalm was read, and another hymn sung ; the Epistle and Gospel being read at the last two wells. The service was now over, and the people dispersed to wander through the village or park, which is thrown open ; the cottagers vie with each other in showing hospitality to the strangers, and many kettles are boiled at their fires, for those who have brought the materials for a picnic on the green. It is welcomed as a season of mirth and good fellow-ship, many old friends meeting there to separate for another year, should they be spared to see the Well-dressing again, whilst the young people enjoy their games and country pastimes with their usual vivacity."

The foregoing account might perhaps furnish us with a model, or hints, for similar excursions in the country.

" Still, Dovedale, yield thy flowers to deck the fountains
    Of Tissington upon its holiday ;
The customs long preserved among the mountains
    Should not be lightly left to pass away ;
They have their moral ; and we often may
    Learn from them how our wise forefathers wrought,
When they upon the public mind would lay
    Some weighty principle, some maxim brought
Home to their hearts, the healthful product of deep thought." —
                                                        Edwards.

The " Pall Mall Budget " of May 23, 1873, says : —

" The town of Buxton last week was the scene of a gay festival, called the Buxton Well Dressing, which took place this year a month earlier than usual. The dressing of one of the wells was, it is stated, a work of art. A lofty arch in front of the well served as the framework of a picture, wrought in flowers, representing a shepherd and his flock. The shepherd's smock was formed of buttercups, the sheep and lambs were made of daisies with pansies for the shades of color, and the ground was rendered in perfect imitation of nature with grasses and moss. The town also was decorated with flowers, and, except the cold east wind; there was no drawback to the success of the whole affair. It seems that this well dressing festival has of late years been substituted for races at Buxton as being more conducive to the general innocence of the inhabitants and visitors, and with the happiest result."

With the view of restoring the Rogation days to their proper use as a season at which the Church beseeches God to bless the coming seed-time and the labors of the husbandman, Bishop Cox, of Western New York, has recently set forth an especial service for these days ; and it has been suggested that others in authority should follow the example, for, if we give thanks for the fruits of the earth in autumn, why should we not, at the proper season, beseech God to bless the labors of the husbandman.

Our New England forefathers observed a somewhat similar custom in their Spring Fast, although their Puritanical severity would not have permitted them to go " processioning."

CHAPTER XV.

WHITSUNTIDE.

HERE is some dispute among the learned as to the meaning of the word Whitsun; it is said by some to have been derived from the custom in the Primitive Church of the catechumens wearing white garments, or chrisoms, at this time, which was then observed as one of the two principal seasons of public baptism. Dr. Neale, however, thinks it curious "that the name *Whitsun-*

day should be thus mistaken. It is neither *White Sunday* (for in truth the color is red), nor *Huit* Sunday, as the *eighth* after Easter; but simply by the various corruptions of the German *Pfingsten*, the Dansk *Pinste*, the various patois *Pingsten*, *Whingsten*, etc., derived from Pentecost." In proof of the above, note that it is not Easter *Sunday*, but Easter *Day*, so it is not Whit *Sunday* but *Whitsun Day;* and we speak of Whitsun Week, just as they do of Pfingsten Woche, in German. Whatever may have been the origin of the term, Whitsuntide has been from the earliest times observed in England, as in Germany, by the celebration of all sorts of outdoor sports and pastimes. It was at this season, also, that the Whitsun Ales were held — those "drinking assemblies" at which parishioners were expected to drink ale for the especial good of their souls; when the church-wardens sold the ale to the populace, in the church-yard, and to the better sort, as it is said, even in the church itself, the profits being set apart (as in our modern fairs) for the repair or decoration of the church, and for the maintenance of the poor. On these occasions were witnessed those exhibitions of archery which once made Old England famous throughout all the world; and also matches at running and wrestling, with other athletic sports. England, as Shakespeare says, was then —

"Busied with a Whitsun morris-dance."

The mummers also appear again with —

"Robin Hood and his merry men all,"

and St. George — who at Christmas was but a carpet knight — now literally "takes the field," or rather *to* the field. Nor was music wanting on these occasions to enliven the sports ; for besides the bells of the morris-dancers, there were the pipe and tabor in modern times, and the harp and viol in the days of more remote antiquity, according to an old ballad : —

"Harke, harke, I heare the dancing,
And a nimble morris-prancing ;
The bagpipe and the morris-bells,
That they are not far hence us tells ;
Come let us all goe thither,
And dance like friends together."

The morris-dance was an essential part of the Whitsun Ale and May Games, and in some places it is still continued as a Whitsuntide amusement. A set consists of six or eight young men, one of whom represents Maid Marian, and another personates the clown or fool, and the remainder are without their coats and waistcoats and in the cleanest and best shirts they can procure, gaily bedizened with pendant ribbons and rosettes of various colors. They often have as many as six rows of bells on their legs. The fool is variously but always grotesquely attired, and carries the usual badge in his hand — an inflated bladder filled with beans, which he rattles about to clear the way for their performances. Maid Marian carries a ladle in her hand with which she solicits money. " The dance consists of a variety of manœuvres, rapid changes of posture, striking first the toe and then the heel on the ground which occasions great jingling of the bells ; repeatedly clapping their hands, then their knees and each other's hands."

It is to us in America an interesting fact, connected with these Whitsuntide observances, that the voyager Sir Humphrey Gilbert, in an expedition fitted out by him under royal commission, sailing from Dartmouth in *June*, 1583, and which planted the first *English* colony west of the Atlantic, " provided," says Mr. Hayes, the historian of the voyage, " for the solace of our own people, and the allurement of the savages, music in good variety, not omitting the least toys, as morris-dancers, hobby-horses, and May-like conceits to delight the savage people."

But before proceeding with an account of the Whitsun Ales, we propose to notice briefly a singular piece of ecclesiastical pageantry formerly connected in popular estimation with the joyous celebration of Whitsuntide.

Previous to the invention of printing, such religious shows were to the people very much what books and pictures are now.

The machinery then used seems ludicrous to us with our superior advantages, but it by no means follows that it was so to them.

Whitsuntide, it appears, was anciently distinguished by a singular display of fireworks of a peculiarly ecclesiastical character, calculated, as was supposed, to represent to the people the descent of the Holy Ghost on the Day of Pentecost.

The " Bee-hive of the Romish Church," satirically speaking of these, says : —

"They send downe a dove out of an owle's nest devised in the roof of the church ; but first they cast out rosin and gunpowder, with wild fire, to make the children afraid, and that must needs be the Holie Ghost which cometh with thunder and lightning."

Perhaps Mr. Fosbrooke's account of this extraordinary spectacle will best exemplify the custom : —

"This feast," says he, "was celebrated in Spain with representations of the gift of the Holy Ghost, and of thunder from engines, which did much damage. Wafers or cakes, preceded by water, oak-leaves, or burning torches, were thrown down from the church roof ; small birds with cakes tied to their legs, and pigeons were let loose ; sometimes there were tame white ones tied with strings, or one of wood suspended. A long censer was also swung up and down."

In the same learned author's "Encyclopædia of Antiquities" we find also the following : —

"In an old computus, Anno 1509, of St. Patrick's, Dublin, we have iv^s vii^d paid to those playing with the great and little angel and the dragon ; iii^s paid for little cords employed about the Holy Ghost ; iv^s vi^d for making the angel (thurifurcantis) censing, and ii^s ii^d for cords of it — all on the Feast of Pentecost."

Lambarde, when a child, saw a like show in St. Paul's Cathedral, London : —

"The descent of the Holy Ghost was performed by a white pigeon being let fly out of a hole in the midst of the roof of the great aisle, with a long censer, which descending from the same place almost to the ground, was swung up and down at such a length, that it reached with one sweep almost to the west-gate of the Church, and with the other to the choir stairs, breathing out over the whole church and the assembled multitude a most pleasant perfume."

Easter Ales and Whitsun Ales, so called from their being held on Easter Sunday and on Whitsunday, or on some of the holidays that follow them, originated from the wakes. These wakes were primitively held upon the day of the dedication of the church, or on the birthday of the saint whose relics were therein deposited, or to whose honor it was consecrated. The

generosity of the founder and endower thereof was at
the same time celebrated, and a service composed suitable to the occasion. This is still done in the Colleges of Oxford, to the memory of the respective
founders. On the eve of this day, prayers were said
and hymns were sung all night in the church; and
from these watchings the festivals were styled " wakes; "
which name still continues in many parts of England,
although the vigils have been long in disuse.

These wakes when first established, it is said, greatly
resembled the Agapæ, or Love-Feasts, of the early
Christians. In process of time, however, the people
assembled on the vigil, or evening preceding the
saint's day, and came, says a quaint old author, " to
churche with candellys burnyng, and would wake,
and come towards night to the churche in their de-
vocion."

The old author above quoted on the subject of
these wakes, mentions certain scandalous excesses into
which the people had gradually fallen, unmindful of an
ancient canon which required that, " Those who came
to the wake should pray devoutly and not betake themselves to drunkenness and debauchery,"—vices to which
it seems our Anglo-Saxon forefathers were always too
much inclined; he says: " And afterwards the people
fell to letcherie and songs, and daunces, with harping
and piping, and also to glotony and sinne; and so
tourned the holyness to cursydness."

Whatsoever truth there may have been in these

serious charges, it is certain that in proportion as
these festivals deviated from the original design of
their institution, they increased in popularity, the con-
viviality was extended, and not only the inhabitants of
the parish to which the church belonged were present
at them, but they were joined by others from the
neighboring towns and parishes.

The church-wardens and other chief officers of the
church, observing these wakes to be more popular
than any other holidays, shrewdly conceived that by
establishing other institutions somewhat similar to
them, they might draw together a large company of
people, and annually collect from them, gratuitously as
it were, such sums of money for the support and
repairs of the church, as would be a great easement
to the parish rates.   By way of enticement to the populace, they brewed a certain portion of strong ale, to
be ready on the day appointed for the festival, which
they sold to them; and most of the better sort, in
addition to what they paid for their drink, contributed
something towards the collection; but in some instances, the inhabitants of one or more parishes were
mulcted in a certain sum, according to mutual agree-
ment, as appears by an ancient stipulation couched in
the following terms : —

"The parishioners of Elvertoon and those of Okebrook in Derbyshire, agree jointly to brew four ales, and every ale of one quarter
of malt, between this and the Feast of St. John the Baptist next

coming, and every inhabitant of the said town of Okebrook shall be
at the several Ales ; and every husband and his wife shall pay two
pence ; and every cottager one penny. And the inhabitants of
Elvertoon shall have and receive all the profits coming of the said
ales, to the use and behoof of the church of Elvertoon ; and the
inhabitants of Elvertoon shall brew eight ales betwixt this and the
Feast of St. John, at which ales the inhabitants of Okebrook shall
come and pay as before rehearsed ; and if any be away one ale, he
is to pay at t'oder ale for both."

Stubbs, on the subject of these ales, says : —

" In certain townes where drunken Bacchus bears sway, against
Christmass and Easter, Whitsunday, or some other time, the church-
wardens — for so they call them — of every parish, with the consent
of the whole parish, provide half a score or twentie quarters of
mault, whereof some they buy of the church stocke, and some is
given to them of the parishioners themselves, every one conferring
somewhat, according to his ability ; which mault being made into
very strong ale, or beer, is set to sale, either in the church, or in
some other place assigned to that. Then, when this nippitatum,
this huffe-cappe, as they call it, this nectar of life, is set abroach,
well is he that can get the soonest to it, and spends the most at it,
for he is counted the godliest man of all the rest, and most in God's
favour, because it is spent upon his church forsooth ! If all be true
which they say, they bestow that money which is got thereby, for
the repair of their churches and chappels ; they buy books for the
service, cupps for the celebration of the Sacrament, surplesses for
Sir John (the parson), and such other necessaries, &c."

In reading the above, some allowance should be
made for the prejudices of Stubbs, who was one of
those puritanical zealots whose reformatory labors in
the succeeding century so disastrously ended in a

general subversion of all things both in Church and State.

However, those more charitably disposed will much prefer the benevolent good humor of honest Old Aubrey, that eminent antiquary of the seventeenth century, whose character for veracity, it is said, has never been impeached : —

" There were no rates for the poor in my grandfather's·days, says he, but for Kingston St. Michael (no small parish) the church ale at Whitsuntide did the business. In every parish is, or was, a church-house, to which belonged spits, crocks, etc., utensils for dressing provisions. Here the housekeepers met and were merry, and gave their charity. The young people were there too, and had dancing, bowling, shooting at butts, etc. ; the ancients sitting gravely by and looking on. All things were civil and without scandal."

At these Whitsun Ales there were chosen a Lord and Lady of Yule, or Ale King and Queen, who were attended by a steward, sword-bearer, purse-bearer, and mace-bearer, with their several badges or ensigns of office. They had, besides, a page or train-bearer, and a jester dressed in a parti-colored jacket ; and with this mock court, they maintained such state and ceremony as their means would permit, presiding over the sports and pastimes of the festival. Sometimes they held this court of theirs in an extensive empty barn or other building suitable for the purpose, extemporized for the occasion into something like an ancient baronial hall.

"The last rural queen of this description," says the "Lancashire Folk Lore," "chosen at Downham, is still living (1867) in Burnley. The lot always fell on these occasions, it is said, to the prettiest girl in the village. A committee of young men made the selection; then it appears an iron crown was procured and dressed with flowers. The King and Queen were ornamented with flowers, a procession was then formed, headed by a fiddler. This proceeded from the inn to the front of 'Squire Asheton's,' Downham Hall, and was composed of javelin men, and all the attendants of royalty. Chairs were brought out of the hall for the King and Queen, ale was handed round, and then a dance was performed on the lawn, the King and Queen leading off. The procession next passed along through the village to the green, where seats were provided for a considerable company. Here again the dancing began, the King and Queen dancing the first set. The afternoon was spent in the usual games, dances, etc. On the next night all the young people met at the inn on invitation from the King and Queen; each paid a shilling towards the 'Queen's Posset.' A large posset was then made and handed round to the company. After this, the evening was spent in dancing and merry-making."

At this season, festivals similar to the above, are still observed in Germany, where it is said:[1]—

"In the country, and among the peasantry everywhere, they dance around the *May-pole* at Whitsuntide, as in England, and maidens awake in the morning to find their windows and doors hung with wreaths of evergreen and flowers, signs of their lovers' truth. Not one but many poles may be seen in every village, dressed from top to bottom, and also little arbors in front of every door, called lovers' bowers, in which they sit and sing, or dance and play. They seek everywhere for this occasion, birchen boughs, and

[1] *Peasant Life in Germany.*

if the festival comes and the leaves of the birch are not yet green, there is great lamentation, and if there is only the slightest appearance of green upon the twigs, they are preferred to all other trees of the forest to hang over the windows and adorn their rooms."

In the rural districts of England, Whitsuntide still continues to be one of the most joyous seasons throughout the year, being chosen for the anniversary of the Clubs and Friendly Societies. Nothing can be more lively and exhilarating than the processioning at these club-holidays; all the attendants dressed in their best, music playing, flags flying, the church bells joining their merry peal, and the whole population of the village coming forth to gaze on the enlivening scene.

CHAPTER XVI.

MAY-DAY.

HE May-day customs are supposed by some antiquarians to have been derived from the Roman Floralia, which began on the twenty-eighth of April, and continued through several days in May. This festival appears to have been instituted about 242 B. C. in honor of a celebrated courtezan named Flora, who bequeathed her fortune to the people of Rome on condition that at this season, they should

yearly celebrate her memory. Soon after, the Senate
of Rome exalted Flora to be the goddess of flowers,
and from that time her festival was observed with various ceremonies, rejoicings, and offering of spring
flowers and branches of trees in bloom.

But Mr. Soane and others maintain that the May-
day festival has come down to us from the Druids,
and that this is proved by many striking facts and co-
incidences, and by none more so than by the vestiges
of the worship of the god Bel, the Apollo or Orus of
other nations. The Druids celebrated his worship on
the first of May, by lighting in honor of him, immense
fires upon the various cairns.

Whether the May-day festival be of Druidical or of
Roman origin, or as Tollet imagines, derived from our
Gothic ancestors, who also welcomed the First of May
with songs and dances, and many rustic sports, appears
to be yet undetermined. Indeed, it has been maintained that its origin is to be sought in far more remote
periods. Maurice says that it is identical with the
Phallic festivals of India and Egypt, which in those
countries took place upon the sun entering Taurus, to
celebrate Nature's renewed fertility.

At any rate, whatever may have been the heathenish
origin of these May-games, the May-pole had become
so firmly rooted in the soil of Merry England long before the time of Charles I., and had been, as was
believed, so thoroughly divested of all its ancient idolatrous associations as to be thought worthy even of

royal and episcopal commendation; its harmless observances being enjoined by the highest ecclesiastical authorities : —

" Our express pleasure therefore is," says King Charles I. (in the "Book of Sports "), " that after the end of Divine Service, our good people be not disturbed, letted, or discouraged from any lawful recreation, such as dancing, either men or women, archery for men, leaping, vaulting, or any other such harmless recreation ; nor from having of May Games, Whitsun Ales, and Morris-dances, and the setting up of May-poles. and other sports therewith used, so as the same be had in due and convenient time, without impediment or neglect of Divine Service."

But whatever may have been the relish with which high church divines read forth to their people from the sacred desk these royal injunctions ; and however much their observance may have been associated with the sentiments of religion and loyalty ; still their celebration, it is well known, gave great offense to that part of their congregations who felt scruples of " conscience" in regard to the use of these games. For in the eyes of our Puritan forefathers, they were simply " heathen abominations." Thus, in response to the King's declaration in the " Book of Sports," we find the defiant puritanical Parliament of 1643 enacting as follows : —

" And because the profanation of the Lord's Day hath been heretofore greatly occasioned by May-poles (a heathenish vanity, generally abused to superstition and wickedness), the Lords and Commons do further order and ordain, that all and singular May-poles, that are or shall be erected, shall be taken down and removed

by the constables, borsholders, tythingmen, petty-constables, and
church-wardens of the parishes where the same be; and that no
May-pole shall be hereafter set up, erected or suffered to be, within
this Kingdom of England, or Dominion of Wales."

In 1661, Thomas Hall, the celebrated non-con-
formist divine, in his " Funebria Floræ, or Downfall
of May-Games," in a solemn arraignment, brings in
twenty arguments in the form of theses against poor
Flora, with a brief dissertation upon each, and ends by
trying her before a packed jury of his own Puritans,
who, as a matter of course, bring her in guilty, when
the parson, as judge, thus pronounces sentence : —

" Flora, thou hast been indicted, by the name of Flora, for bringing in abundance of misrule and disorder into Church and State;
thou hast been found guilty, and art condemned both by God and
man, by Scriptures, fathers, councils, by learned and pious divines,
both old and new, and therefore I adjudge thee to perpetual banishment."

Old Stubbs, also, as usual, is extremely eloquent on
this subject : —

" Against Maie Whitsondaie, or some other tyme of the yeare,
every parishe, toune or village, assemble themselves together, bothe
men women and children, olde and young, even all indifferently ;
and either goyng alltogether, or devyding themselves into companies,
they goe some to the woods and groves, &c., some to the hilles and
mountaines, some to one place, some to an other, where they spende
all the night in pleasant pastymes; and in the mornyng they
returne, bringing with them birch boughs and braunches of trees to
deck their assemblies withall. And no marvaile ; for there is a

great lord present amongst them as superintendent and lorde over their pastymes and sportes ; namely, Sathan, prince of Hell. But their chiefest jewell they bring from thence is their *Maie-pole*, which they bring home with great veneration, as thus : they have twentie or fourtie yoke of oxen, every oxe havying a swete nosegaie of flowers tyed on the tippe of his hornes, and these oxen drawe home this Maie-pole — this stinking idoll rather — which is covered all over with flowers and herbes bounde rounde aboute with stringes, from the top to the bottome, and sometyme painted with variable colours (black and yellow), with twoo or three hundred men women and children followyng it with great devotion. And this beyng reared up, with handkerchiefes and flagges streamyng on the toppe, they strawe the grounde aboute, beside green boughes aboute it; set up summer haulles, bowers and arbours hard by it, and then fall they to banquet and feast, to leap and daunce about it, as the heathen people did at the dedication of their idolles, whereof this is a proper patterne, or rayther the thynge itself."

It is curious enough to contrast the effusions of this rabid fanatic, with the pleasing picture of the same custom left to us by Stowe : —

" In the moneth of May," says the cheerful old man, " namely on May-day in the morning, every man, except impediment, would walk into the sweete meadows and green woods, there to rejoyce their spirites, with the beauty and savour of sweete flowers, and with the harmony of birds praysing God in their kind ; and for example hereof Edward Hall hath noted that K. Henry the Eight, as in the 3 of his reigne and divers other years, so namely on the seventh of his reigne on May-day in the morning with Queene Katheren his wife, accompanied with many Lords and Ladies, rode a Maying from Greenwitch to the high ground of Shooter's hill, where as they passed by the way, they espied a company of tall yeomen clothed all in Greene, with greene whoodes and with bowes and arrowes to the number of 200. One being their chieftaine was called Robin Hoode, who required the king and his companie to stay and see his men shoote, whereunto the king graunting, Robin Hoode whistled, and all the 200 archers shot off, losing all at once; and when he whistled againe, they likewise shot againe; their arrowes whistled by craft of the head, so that the noyse was strange and loude, which greatly delighted the king, queene and their companie. Moreover, this Robin Hoode desired the king and queene, with their retinue, to enter the greene wood, where, in harbours made of boughes and decked with flowers, they were set and served plentifully with venison and wine by Robin Hoode and his meynie, to their great contentment, and had other pageants and pastimes."

"I find also, that in the moneth of May, the citizens of London, of all estates, lightly in every parish, or sometimes two or three parishes joyning togither, had their several Mayings, and did fetch in May-poles, with divers warlike shewes, with good archers, moricedaunrers, and other devices, for pastime all the day long, and towards the evening they had stage playes and bonefires in the streetes. Of these Mayings we reade, in the raigne of Henry the Sixt, that the aldermen and shiriffes of London being, on May-day, at the Bishop of London's wood, in the parish of Stebunheath, and having there a worshipfull dinner for themselves and other commers, Lydgate the poet, that was a monk of Bury, sent to them by a pursivant a joyfull commendation of that season, containing sixteen staves in meter royall, beginning thus: —

> "Mightie Flora, goddesse of fresh bowers,
>   Which clothed hath the soyle in lustie greene,
> Made buds spring, with her sweete showers,
>   By influence of the sunny-shien."

The custom of gathering May-dew survived until the end of the seventeenth century: — "young ladies and even grave matrons, repaired to the fields to gather May-dew with which to beautify their complexions; milkmaids also danced in the streets with their pails wreathed with garlands, and a fiddler going before them."

A hundred years ago " the milk-maids' *garland* was a pyramidal frame, covered with damask, glittering on each side with [borrowed] polished silver plate, and adorned with knots of gay-coloured ribbons and posies of fresh flowers, surmounted with a silver urn or tankard. It was placed on a wooden horse, and carried by two men, preceded by a pipe and tabor or a fiddle."

A good idea of the hilarity of the occasion may be gathered from a curious old ballad in the " Westminster Drollery," called the " Rural Dance about the Maypole :" —

> "Come lasses and lads, take leave of your dads,
>   And away to the May-pole hie ;
> For every *he* has got him a *she*,
>   And the minstrel is standing by ;
> For Willy has gotten his Jill, and Johnny has got his Joan,
> To jig it, jig it, jig it, jig it up and down.
>
> " ' Strike up,' says Wat. ' Agreed,' says Kate,
>   And, ' I prithee, fiddler, play ; '
> ' Content,' says Hodge, and so says Madge,
>   ' For this is a holiday ! '
> Then every man did put his hat off to his lass,
> And every girl did curchy, curchy, curchy on the grass.
>
> " ' Begin,' says Hall. ' Aye, aye,' says Mall,
>   ' We'll lead up *Packington's Pound :*
> ' No, no,' says Noll ; and so says Doll,

' We'll first have *Sellenger's Round.'*
Then every man began to foot it round about,
And every girl did jet it, jet it, jet it in and out.

" ' You're out,' says Dick.   ' 'Tis a lie,' says Nick ;
   ' The fiddler played it false ; '
' 'Tis true,' says Hugh ; and so says Sue,
   And so says nimble Alse.
The fiddler then began to play the tune again,
And every girl did trip it, trip it, trip it to the men."

The morris-dance, the peculiar sport and pastime of
May-day and Whitsuntide, is generally supposed to
be of Moorish origin, derived from Spain.   Hence its
name.   In confirmation of this opinion, we are told by
Junius, that at one time the dancers blackened their
faces to resemble Moors.   Strutt, indeed, thinks differ-
ently ; but his arguments, which are not very strong
in themselves, seem to be altogether set aside by the
fact of the word *morris* being applied in the same way
by other nations to express a dance, that both English
and foreign glossaries alike ascribe to the Moors.
That the dance is not exactly the same as the fan-
dango, the real Morisco, can by no means be considered as invalidating this argument, for similar devi-
ations from originals have taken place in other borrowed amusements.

From whatever source the morris-dance may have
been derived, it would seem to have been first brought
into England about the time of Edward III., when
John of Gaunt returned from Spain.   It was certainly

popular in France, as early as the fifteenth century, under the name of Morisque, which is an intermediate step between the Spanish *Morisco* and the English *morris*. There does not appear to be any mention of this dance by English writers or records before the sixteenth century; but then, and especially in the writers of the Shakespearean age, the allusions to it become very numerous. It was probably introduced into England by dancers both from Spain and France; for in the earlier allusions to it in English, it is sometimes called the Morisco and sometimes the Morisce or Morisk.

Tabourot, the oldest and most curious writer on the art of dancing, says, that in his youthful days, about the beginning of the sixteenth century, it was the custom in good society for a boy to come into the hall when supper was finished, with his face blackened, his forehead bound with white or yellow taffeta, and bells tied to his legs. He then proceeded to dance the Morisco, the whole length of the hall backward and forward, to the great amusement of the company. This was the ancient and uncorrupted morris-dance.

In England, however, it seems to have been very soon united with an older pageant-dance, performed at certain periods in honor of Robin Hood and his outlaws; and thus a morris-dance consisted of a certain number of characters limited at one time to five, but varying considerably at different periods.

There was preserved in an ancient mansion at Bet-

ley, in Staffordshire, some years ago, and it may exist
there still, a painted glass window of apparently the
reign of Henry VIII., representing in its different
compartments the several characters of the morris-
dance. George Tollett, Esq., who possessed the mansion at the beginning of this century, and who was
a friend of the Shakespearean critic Malone, gave a
lengthy dissertation on this window, with an engraving.
Maid Marian, the Queen of May, is there dressed in a
rich costume of the period referred to, with a golden
crown on her head, and a red pink in her left hand,
supposed to be intended as the emblem of Summer : —

" This Queen of May is supposed to represent the goddess Flora
of the Roman festival ; Robin Hood appears as the lover of the
Maid Marian. An ecclesiastic also appears among the characters
in the window, in the full clerical tonsure, with a chaplet of red and
white beads in his right hand ; his corded girdle and his russet
habit denoting him to be of the Franciscan order, or one of the
Gray Friars ; his stockings are red ; his red girdle is ornamented
with a golden twist and with a golden tassel."

This is supposed to be Friar Tuck, a well-known
character of the Robin Hood ballads. The Fool,
with his cock's comb and bauble, also takes his place
in the figures in the window; neither is the taborer
wanting with his tabor and pipe, " nor has the hobby-
horse been forgot." [1]

[1] At Banbury there is annually exhibited a pageant, in which a fine lady on a
white horse, preceded by Robin Hood and Little John, Friar Tuck, a company of
archers, bands of music, flags and banners, passes through the principal street to

We may infer from the extraordinary longevity of those skilled in the morris-dances, that the exercise was conducive to the health of the body at least, if not equally so to that of the soul; the believers in "muscular Christianity," however, may reasonably doubt whether what was so good for the body, could be after all, as the Puritans maintained it was, so very bad for the soul.

Sir William Temple thus mentions a morris-dance which took place in Herefordshire, in King James' time : —

"There went about the country a sett of Morrice dancers, composed of ten men, who danced a Maid Marrian, and a tabor and pipe ; these ten, one with one another made up twelve hundred years. Tis not so much that so many in one country should live to that age, as that they should be in vigor and humour to travel and dance."

About a century ago, also, a famous May-game or morris-dance, was performed by eight men in the same county, whose ages computed together amounted to eight hundred years.

Brady, in his " Clavis Calendaria," published in London in 1812, says of "the May Pole, that it is still retained in most of our villages," and that, "the May-

the Cross, where the lady (Maid Marian) scatters Banbury cakes among the people. This Cross, so celebrated in the nursery hymn, "Ride a cock horse to Banbury Cross," pulled down by the Puritans in the reign of Elizabeth, has recently been rebuilt by the Banburians, to commemorate the marriage of the Princess Royal with the Crown Prince of Prussia.

games were also once so general in England, that even
the priests,[1] joining with the people, used to go in procession to some adjoining wood on the May morning,
and return in triumph with the much prized pole,
adorned with boughs, flowers, and other tokens of the
Spring season."

> " Happy the age, and harmless were the days
>   (For then true love and amity was found),
> When every village did a May-pole raise,
>   And Whitsun Ales and May-games did abound ;
> And all the lusty yonkers, in a rout,
>   With merry lasses daunc'd the rod about ;
> Then Friendship to their banquets bid the guests,
> And poore men far'd the better for their feasts.

> " The lords of castles, mannors, towns, and towers,
>   Rejoic'd when they beheld the farmers flourish,
> And would come downe unto the summer bowers,
>   To see the country gallants daunce the morrice."

The May-pole, once fixed, remained until the end of
the year, and was resorted to at all other seasons of
festivity, as well as during May. Hence the general
term of " May-games," to which reference is made in
the " Book of Sports " and other contemporaneous writings. Some of these poles, made of wood of a more
durable nature, remained for years, being merely

---

[1] Dr. Parr was a great patron of May-day festivities. Opposite his parsonage
house at Watton near Warwick, stood the parish May-pole, which was annually
dressed with garlands, and the doctor himself danced with his parishioners
around the shaft.

freshly ornamented instead of being removed, as was
the common practice. The last of such permanent
May-poles in London was taken down in 1717, and
conveyed to Wanstead, in Essex, where it was fixed in
the park for the support of an immensely large tel-
escope. Its original height was upward of one hundred feet above the surface of the ground, and its
station on the east side of Somerset House has been
thus commemorated by Pope: —

> " Amidst the area wide they took their stand,
>   Where the tall May-pole once o'erlook'd the Strand."

The May-pole in later times in this country, appears
to have been transformed into the Liberty-pole.

The third canto of Trumbull's " McFingal" is
called the " Liberty-Pole." When the hero caught
sight of it and the crowd around it, he exclaimed : —

> " What mad-brained rebel gave commission
>   To raise this *May-pole* of sedition."

We may infer from the above that Trumbull
thought that the May-pole, around which in England young people had joyful gatherings, suggested
our Liberty-pole first raised in New York, in 1766, and
which has been erected in all parts of this country as a
rallying point for public meetings and Fourth of July
celebrations.

Another May-day custom worthy of notice, is still

kept up at Oxford. On the top of the magnificent tower of Magdalen College, an anthem is sung at sunrise every May morning. The choristers and singing men of the College Chapel in their surplices, assemble there a little before five o'clock, and as soon as the clock has struck, commence singing their matins.

The college, it appears, holds certain land on condition of the annual performance of this ceremony, which, by the way, is said to be a substitute for a mass or requiem, which before the Reformation used to be annually sung in the same exalted position, for the rest of the soul of Henry VII. the founder of the college. The beautiful bridge, and all around the college, is covered with spectators, the inhabitants of the city as well as the neighboring villages collecting together, some on foot, and some in carriages, to hear the choir, and welcome in the happy day. The effect of the singing is said to be sweet and solemn, and almost supernatural, and during its celebration the most profound stillness reigns over the assembled numbers; all seem impressed with the angelic softness of the floating sounds, as they are gently wafted down by each breath of air. All is hushed and calm and quiet — even breathing is almost forgotten, and all seem lost even to themselves, until with the first peal of the bells (of which there are ten) the spell is broken, and noise and confusion usurp the place of silence and quiet.

CHAPTER XVII.

ST. JOHN'S, OR MIDSUMMER'S EVE.

HE history of the Holidays would be incomplete without a brief account of those brilliant festivities celebrated in days of yore on St. John's, or Midsummer's Eve.

The festival of the Baptist has been from the earliest time one of the most popular of holidays.

The observances connected with the Nativity of St. John commenced on the previous evening, called as usual the Eve, or Vigil of the festival, or Midsummer Eve.

At this time people were accustomed to go into the woods and break down branches of trees, which they brought to their homes and planted over their doors, making therewith their " housis gay into remembrance of St. John the Baptist, and of this that was prophecied of him, that manye schoulden joy in his burthe."

This custom was universal in England till the recent change in manners. In Oxford there was a specialty in the observance, of a curious nature. Within the first court of Magdalen College, from a stone pulpit at a corner, a sermon used to be preached on St. John's Day ; at the same time the court was embowered with green boughs and flowers, that the preaching might resemble that of the Baptist in the wilderness.

It appears from the records of the college that payment for these decorations was made for the last time in the year 1766, for the old custom of preaching an annual sermon from the stone pulpit in the quadrangle was then transferred to the chapel, "for fear," says Whitefield, " it may be they should give further sanction to field preaching," which the Methodists had at that time already begun.

The Nativity of St. John the Baptist occurring at the summer solstice, the holiday observances peculiar to the season naturally became mixed up with those of the more primitive festival.[1]

---

[1] "The Pagan rites of this festival at the summer solstice may be considered as a counterpart of those used at the winter solstice at Yule-tide. . . . . In the old Runic Fasti, a wheel was used to denote the festival of Christmas. . . . . This wheel is common to both festivities." — *Brand.*

Among these customs that of lighting fires on Midsummer Eve is the most ancient and widely spread. In early times these were kindled on eminences marked by heaps of stone or carnes consecrated to the worship of Baal the Sun-god.

Gebelin, a learned historian and antiquary, in his " Allegories Orientales," says that " the St. John Fires " were kindled about midnight on the very moment of the solstice by the greater part as well of ancient as of modern nations ; it was a religious ceremony of the most remote antiquity, which was observed for the prosperity of states and people, and to dispel every kind of evil ! " The origin of this fire, which is still retained by so many nations, though enveloped in the mist of antiquity, is very simple : it was a Feu de Joie, kindled the very moment the year began, for the first of all years, and the most ancient that we know of, began at this month of June. Thence the very name of this month, junior, the *youngest*, which is renewed; while that of the preceding one is May, major, the ancient. Thus the one was the month of young people, while the other belonged to old men. These Feux de Joie were accompanied at the same time with vows and sacrifices for the prosperity of the people and the fruits of the earth. They danced also round this fire (for what feast is there without a dance?) and the most active leaped over it. Each on departing took away a fire-brand, great or small, and the remains were scattered to the wind, which at the same time that it dispersed the ashes, was thought to expel every evil." These bon-fires or bone fires, as they were generally called, were formerly believed to be a potent antidote against evil spirits. The old Homily "*De Festo Sancti Johannis Baptistæ*" says : "Wyse clerkes knoweth well that dragons hate nothyng more than the stenche of brennynge bones, and therefore they gaderyd as many as they might fynde and brent them; and so with the stenche thereof they drove away the dragons, and so they were brought out of greete dysease."

The custom of lighting fires on St. John's Eve was commonly observed in Ireland until a very recent period. A writer in the "Gentleman's Magazine" for February, 1795, observes : —

"I was so fortunate in the summer of 1782, as to have my curiosity gratified by the sight of this ceremony to a very great extent of country. At the house where I was entertained, it was told me that we should see at midnight the most singular sight in Ireland, which was *the lighting of fires in honour of the sun*. Accordingly, exactly at midnight, the fires began to appear ; and taking the advantage of going up to the leads of the house, I saw on a radius of thirty miles, all around, the fires burning on every eminence which the country afforded. I had a farther satisfaction in learning from undoubted authority, that the people *danced round the fires*, and at the close went through these fires, and made their sons and daughters, together with their cattle pass through the fire ; and the whole was conducted with religious solemnity."

A kindred custom peculiar to this season was that of keeping a watch during the Midsummer Night, although no such practice might prevail at the place from mere motives of precaution. This custom was observed at Nottingham, as late as the reign of Charles I. Every citizen either went himself or sent a substitute, and an oath for preservation of peace was duly administered to the company at their first meeting at sunset. They paraded the town in parties during the night, every person wearing a garland of flowers upon his head, additionally embellished, in some instances, with ribbons and jewels. " This custom of wearing floral crowns appears to have been very general in old times, not only on St. John's Day, but also on other festive occasions."

Polydore Virgil says, that in England they not only decorated the church with flowers, but the priests, crowned with flowers, performed the service on certain high days, more especially at St. Paul's Cathedral in London, on the feast day of the patron Saint.

Stow records that in his time the ritualistic dean and chapter of that cathedral on St. Paul's Day, were " appareled in copes and vestments with garlands of roses on their heads."

" A probable relic of this custom may be traced in the fact that the judges, the Lord Mayor, the aldermen, sheriffs, and common councillors, when they attend service in great state at the cathedral on the Sunday after Easter, and on Trinity Sunday, with many of the clergy, carry each of them a boquet of flowers in their hands."

In London, on St. John's Eve, or Midsummer Night, the people illuminated their houses with clusters of

lamps, and performed the ceremony of setting the city
watch with great show and splendor.   The watchmen
were clothed for the occasion in bright harness ; the
Lord Mayor, the city officers, and a crowd of minstrels,
henchmen, giants, pageants, and morris-dancers, formed
part of the procession, over which a flood of light was
poured from hundreds of blazing cressets and huge
torches carried upon men's shoulders.

This general illumination and rejoicing doubtless
had some reference to the Baptist; the illumination
and festivity being suggested by the text, " He was a
burning and a shining light; and ye were willing for
a season to rejoice in his light." (John v. 35.)

Pageants of all kinds were very popular at this time
in different towns, and in none more so than in the
ancient city of Chester, where the Whitsuntide festivities seem to have embraced those of the proximate
red-letter Day of St. John the Baptist.   In the 24th
Henry VIII. there was issued a proclamation made by
William Nowall, clerk of the pendice, setting forth
that : —

" In ould tyme not only for the augmentacyon and increes of the
holy and catholick faith, and to exhort the minds of common people
to good devotion and wholesome doctrine, but also for the common-
wealthe and prosperity of this citty (Chester), a play and declaracyon
of divers stories of the Bible, beginning with the creation and fall
of Lucifer, and ending with the generall judgment of the world, to
be declared and played openly in pageants in the Whitsonne weeke,
was devised and made by Sir Henry Francis, somtyme mooncke

there ; who gat of Clement then bushop of Rome, 1000 days of pardon, and of the bushop of Chester at that tyme 40 days of pardon, to every person resorting in peaceable manner to see and heare the said plays ; which were, to the honor of God, by John Arnway, then Mayor of Chester, his brethren, and the whole cominalty thereof, to be brought forth declared and played at the coste and charges of the craftsmen and occupacyons of the said city," etc.

All who disturbed them were to be accursed of the Pope till he absolved them.

The setting of the "watch" on St. John's Eve at Chester, appears to have been a very showy exhibition, which at one time was greatly objected to on the alleged score of immorality ; but this objection was overruled by the anti-puritanical authorities of Queen Elizabeth's time : " Four giants, one unicorn, one dromedary, one luce, one camel, one ass, one dragon, six hobby-horses, and sixteen naked boys," were included in the pageants. At this time (1564) it appears that such quantities of pasteboard cloth and other materials were required for building up the giants to a proper size, that these alone cost five pounds a head, equal to three times that amount at the present day. Another of the items is still more curious: " Two shillings' worth of arsenic " had to be mixed with the paste to save the giants from being devoured by the rats.

Strutt remarks that pageants, though commonly exhibited in the great towns and cities of England on solemn and joyous occasions, were more frequent in London than elsewhere on account of its being the theatre for the entertainment of foreign monarchs, and for the procession of the kings and queens to their coronation. At the coronation of Queen Elizabeth on Sunday, January 15th, 1559, her progress was marked by superb pageants. On her arrival at Temple Bar, Gog and Magog,[1] two giants, those famous worthies of Guildhall memory, were seen holding above the gate a table, wherein was written in Latin verse the effect of all the pageants which the city before had erected.

The most popular part of these shows was the figures of the giants and dragons, which down even to a very recent period were carried about in the civic processions both in England and on the Continent.

In some places these shows were condemned by the ecclesiastical authorities as opposed to the spirit of Christianity, being, according to the mandate of the Archbishop of Arras (1699), " only fit to provoke the

---

[1] The two " terrible " giants, Gog and Magog, " had the honor yearly to grace my Lord Mayor's show, being carried in great triumph in the time of the pageants, and when that eminent annual service was over, remounted their old stations in Guildhall, till by reason of their very great age, old time, with the help of a number of city rats and mice had eaten up all their entrails. The dissolution of the two old weak and feeble giants gave birth to the two present substantial and majestic giants ; who by order, and at the city charge, were formed and fashioned. . . . . and were immediately advanced to their lofty stations in Guildhall, which they have peaceably enjoyed ever since the year 1708. — " *Gog and Magog,*" *Fairholt.*

" Some few modern attempts have been made to resuscitate the old pageants. In 1837, two colossal figures of the Guildhall Giants walked in the procession."

wrath of God," and yet they seem once to have had a religious signification, the giants and dragons typifying the powers of earth and hell, subjugated and chained to the chariot wheels of triumphant Christianity.

In England, in the time of the Commonwealth, the giants together with the images of the beasts exhibited were destroyed, but at the Restoration of Charles the Second it was agreed by the citizens to replace the pageant as usual on the Eve of St. John the Baptist.

At this season of public rejoicing the fronts of houses in the streets through which the processions passed were covered with rich adornments of tapestry, arras, and cloth of gold; the chief magistrates and most opulent citizens usually appeared on horseback in sumptuous habits, and joined the cavalcade, while the ringing of bells, the sound of music from various quarters, and the shouts of the populace, nearly stunned the ears of the spectators.

The encouragement that literature and the Greek language received from Queen Elizabeth, created a fashion for classical allusions upon every convenient occasion, and the Queen's admiration of this kind of compliment, caused the mythology of ancient learning to be introduced into the various shows and spectacles in her honor. Wharton says, that when she paraded through a country town, almost every pageant was a pantheon. When she paid a visit at the house of any of her nobility, on entering the hall she was saluted by the Penates, and conducted to her privy-chamber by Mercury : in the afternoon, when she condescended to walk in the garden, the lake was covered with tritons and nereids ; the pages of the family were converted into wood-nymphs, who passed from every bower ; and the footmen gamboled over the lawn in the figure of satyrs.

To conclude this subject we give a very graphic and characteristic description, by a poet of the seventeenth century (1616), of a London marching watch on St. John's Eve. There is something grand and sublime in the idea of thus heralding in, as it were, the Nativity of the Baptist, at whose birth it was said "many shall rejoice," and who was the destined fore-runner of Him "whose goings forth have been of old," and whose kingdom was to be "an everlasting kingdom, that all people, nations, and languages should serve him : " —

"The wakeful shepherd by his flock in field,
    With wonder at that time far off beheld
    The wanton shine of thy triumphant fiers,
    Playing upon the tops of thy tall spiers :
    Thy goodly buildings, that till then did hide
    Their rich array, open'd their windowes wide,
    Where kings, great peeres, and many a noble dame,
    Whose bright, pearl-glittering robes did mock the flame
    Of the night's burning lights did sit to see
    How every senator, in his degree
    Adorn'd with shining gold and purple weeds,
    And stately mounted on rich trapped steeds,
    Their guard attending, through the streets did ride

Before their foot-bands, graced with glittering pride
Of rich-guilt armes, whose glory did present
A sunshine to the eye, as if it meant
Amongst the cresset lights shot up on hie,
To chase darke night for ever from the skie,
While in the streets the stickelers to and fro,
To keep decorum, still did come and go ;
While tables set were plentifully spread,
And at each doore neighbor with neighbor fed."[1]

There are many superstitions of heathen origin connected with the observances of St. John's Day. Henderson in his "Folk Lore of the Northern Counties of
England," says that : —

"From the beginning, the Church appears practically to have tolerated such parts of the old mythological system as she considered
harmless, and to have permitted them to live on without check or
rebuke. The mass of the clergy also being of the people, were consequently imbued with the same prejudices, feelings, and superstitions as those to whom they ministered." "Perfectly unacquainted
with the laws that govern the universe, the early Christians, like
the Pagans and Neo-Platonists, made supernatural beings the special
cause of all the phenomena of Nature. They attributed to these
beings, according to their beneficial or injurious effects, all atmos-
pheric phenomena ; according to them, angels watched over the
different elements, and demons endeavored to overthrow their
power."

The early Fathers of the Church, in their controversy with their Pagan opponents, did not deny the
existence of these "gods," but rather maintained the
Scriptural doctrine that the gods which the heathen

---

[1] For Stow's account of the Marching Watch, see Appendix.

worshipped were in reality demons or devils: "They sacrificed unto devils, not to God ; to gods whom they knew not." (Deut. xxxii. 17.) The conversion of our heathen ancestors to Christianity, it seems, was not so complete as to have entirely eradicated their belief in the influence and power of their ancient deities. Hence the still popular belief in omens, divinations, and enchantments of different kinds, especially those formerly practiced at the summer solstice.[1]

Durand, speaking of the rites of the Feast of St. John the Baptist, informs us of this curious circumstance ; that in some places they roll a wheel about, to signify that the sun, then occupying the highest place in the zodiac, is beginning to descend. And in the amplified account of these ceremonies given by the poet Naogeorgius, we read that this wheel was taken up to the top of a mountain and rolled down from thence ; and that, as it had been previously covered with straw twisted about it and set on fire, it appeared at a distance as if the sun had been falling from the sky. And he further observes, that the people imagine that all their ill-luck rolls away from them together with this wheel.

But all such practices as these were strictly forbidden by the early Fathers, and by the general and pro-

---

[1] It is said that almost if not quite up to the present time, on holiday eves, the Norwegian peasant offered cakes, sweet porridge, and libations of wort or buttermilk, on mounds consecrated to the invisible folk, and called "bœttir mounds."

vincial councils of the Church, on the ground that they were in reality an appeal to the false gods of their ancestors.

The influence of demons seems to have been thought by the superstitious to be especially great on the eve of the Nativity of the Baptist, who was declared by the Scripture to be the forerunner of Him who was to be the destroyer of the " Prince of the power of the air," and of all the "powers of darkness;" hence the rage of devils and evil spirits on this night.

The disturbed state of the air made it unsafe to sleep, for the demons had the power to separate soul and body temporarily, transporting the spirit, by a fearful nightmare, as it were, to the place where soul and body should finally be separated; hence, also, the Marching Watch, with its literal application of the words of St. Paul: " Put on the whole armor of God that ye may be able to stand against the wiles of the devil. For we wrestle not against flesh and blood, but against principalities, against powers, against the rulers of the darkness of this world."

The use of material fire in combating spiritual enemies has been thus satirized by the author of the " Comical Pilgrim's Pilgrimage in Ireland," 1725 : —

" On the Vigil of St. John the Baptist's Nativity, they make bonfires, and run along the streets and fields with wisps of straw blazing on long poles, to purify the air, which they think infectious, by believing all the devils, spirits, ghosts, and hobgoblins fly abroad this night to hurt mankind."

The popular superstition in regard to Christmas Eve is in pleasing contrast to the foregoing direful picture of the spiritual condition of Ireland : —

> " And then, they say, no spirit can walk abroad ;
> The nights are wholesome ; then no planets strike,
> No fairy takes, nor witch hath power to charm ;
> So hallowed and so gracious is the time." — *Shakespeare.*

The author quoted, on the superstitions of Ireland, thus continues his account with great disgust : " Furthermore, it is their dull theology to affirm the souls of all people leave their bodies on the eve of this feast, and take their ramble. to that very place, where, by land or sea, a final separation shall divorce them for evermore in this world."

Are not the spirit-rappings and table-turnings of these days a return to something like a belief in demonology and witchcraft ? and may we not expect that hobgoblins and sprites will yet be conjured up from the depths of that Red Sea to which they have been consigned by the exorcisms of our forefathers ?

The belief in the unseen world, and in the powers of darkness on this particular eve, was once very general in most countries.

Washington Irving refers to the superstition in the " Alhambra," in the legend of Governor Manco and the Soldier.   All Spain is declared by the story-teller to be —

> " A country under the power of enchantment.   There is not a
> mountain cave, not a lonely watch-tower in the plains, nor ruined

castle on the hills, but has some spell-bound warriors sleeping from age to age within its vaults, until the sins are expiated for which Allah permitted the dominion to pass for a time out of the hands of the faithful. Once every year, on the Eve of St. John, they are released from enchantment from sunset to sunrise, and permitted to repair here to pay homage to their sovereign Boabdil; and the crowds which you beheld swarming into the cavern are Moslem warriors, from their haunts in all parts of Spain."

In the Neapolitan towns, says the author of "Roba di Roma" —

"Great fires are built on this festival, around which the people dance, jumping through the flames, and flinging themselves about in every wild and fantastic attitude. And if you would have a medicine to cure all wounds and cuts, go out before daylight, and pluck the little flower called *pilatro* (St. John's wort), and make an infusion of it before the sun is up; but at all events, be sure on the eve of this day to place a plate of salt at the door, for it is the witches' festival, and no one of the tribe can pass the salt to injure you without first counting every grain, a task which will occupy the whole night, and thus save you from evil. Besides this, place a pitchfork, or any fork, by the door, as an additional safeguard, in case she calls in allies to help her count."

In Germany, on St. John's Eve, says Thorpe, the witches are believed to hold their meetings, at which they eat the berries of the mountain-ash; and on St. John's Day the Divining rod must be cut from a hazel backwards.

Among the enchantments which were once practiced on Midsummer Eve, by young maidens in search of suitable partners for life, was that of gathering for magical purposes the rose, St. John's wort (*Hypericum pulcrum*), vervanis, trefoil, rue, and fern seed (it was thought that to possess this seed, not easily visible, was a means of rendering one's self invisible). Young women likewise sought for what they called pieces of coal, but in reality, certain hard, black, dead roots, often found under the living mugwort, designing to place these under their pillows, that they might dream of their lovers. Says Aubrey : —

"The last summer, on the day of St. John Baptist (1694), I accidentally was walking in the pasture behind Montague House ; it was twelve o'clock. I saw there about two or three and twenty young women, most of them well habited, on their knees very busie, as if they had been weeding. I could not presently learn what the matter was ; at last a young man told me that they were looking for a coal under the root of a plantain, to put under their heads that night, and they should dream who would be their husbands. It was to be found that day and hour."

We may suppose from the following version of a German poem, entitled the "St. John's Wort," that precisely the same notions prevail amongst the peasant youth of Germany : —

"The young maid stole through the cottage door,
And blush'd as she sought the plant of power:
'Thou silver glow-worm, O lend me thy light,
I must gather the mystic St. John's wort to-night —
The wonderful herb, whose leaf will decide
If the coming year will make me a bride.'

And the glow-worm came
With its silvery flame,
And sparkled and shone
Through the night of St. John.
And soon has the young maid her love-knot tied.
With noiseless tread,
To her chamber she sped,
Where the spectral moon her white beams shed ;
' Bloom here, bloom here, thou plant of power,
To deck the young bride in her bridal hour !'
But it droop'd its head, that plant of power,
And died the mute death of the voiceless flower ;
And a withered wreath on the ground it lay,
More meet for a burial than bridal day.
And when a year was past away,
All pale on her bier the young maid lay ;
And the glow-worm came
With its silvery flame,
And sparkled and shone
Through the night of St. John,
As they closed the cold grave o'er the maid's cold clay."

The Orpine plant, sometimes called "midsummer man," also occurs among the following love divinations on Midsummer Eve, preserved in the "Connoisseur:"—

"I and my two sisters tried the dumb cake together ; you must know, two must make it, two bake it, two break it, and the third put it under each of their pillows (but you must not speak a word all the time) and then you will dream of the man you are to have. This we did, and, to be sure, I did nothing all night but dream of Mr. Blossom. The same night exactly at twelve o'clock, I sowed hemp-seed in our back yard, and said to myself : ' Hemp-seed I sow,[1] hemp-seed I hoe, and he that is my true love come after me and mow.' Will you believe me? I looked back and saw him as plain as eyes could see him. After that I took a clean shift and wetted it, and turned it wrong side out, and hung it to the fire upon the back of a chair; and very likely my sweetheart would have come and turned it right again (for I heard his step), but I was frightened, and could not help speaking, which broke the charm. I myself stuck up two midsummer men, one for myself and one for him. Now if his had died away, we should never have come together; but I assure you his bowed and turned to mine. Our maid Betty tells me, if I go backwards, without speaking a word, into the garden upon Midsummer Eve, and gather a rose, and keep it in a clean sheet of paper, without looking at it till Christmas Day, it will be as fresh as in June; and if I then stick it in my bosom, he that is to be my husband will come and take it out."

A proof of the antiquity and universality of these popular superstitions is to be found in a ring, recently discovered in a ploughed field near Cawood, in York-shire, which appeared from the style of its inscription to be of the fifteenth century. It bore for a device, *two orpine plants* joined by a true-love-knot, with this motto above, "*Ma fiancée velt,*" that is my sweetheart wills, or is desirous. The stalks of the plants were bent toward each other, in token, no doubt, that the parties represented by them were to come together

---

[1] The same superstition is referred to in Burns' *Halloween* : —

> " Hemp-seed, I saw thee ;
> An' her that is to be my lass,
> Come after me, and draw thee
> As fast this night."

in marriage. The motto under the ring was "*Joye l'amour feu.*"

From the first, says Mr. Henderson, the Church by the decrees of councils and the voice of her chief fathers and doctors condemned such superstitions (as we have noticed above), not however on the ground of their folly, but of their impiety. It is possible, therefore, that her denunciations might go toward confirming a belief in the minds of the people in the whole fabric of superstition, as a real and powerful though forbidden thing — the " Black Art," as it was called.

A long list of popular superstitions was condemned by a council held in the eighth century at Leptines in Hainault. Pope Gregory III. also issued similar anathemas. The Capitularies of Charlemagne and his successors, repeat the denunciations of them.

About the same date similar superstitions were rebuked in Scotland by the Abbot Cameanus the Wise. In the same century, St. Eligius, Bishop of Nayon, preached against similar superstitions : —

"Above all, I implore you not to observe the sacrilegious customs of the Pagans. Do not consult the gravers of talismans, nor diviners, nor sorcerers, nor enchanters, for any sickness whatsoever. Do not take notice of auguries, or of sneezings ; do not pay attention to the songs of the birds when you go abroad. Let no Christian pay regard to the particular day on which he leaves a house or enters it. Let no one perplex himself about the new moon or eclipses. Let no one do on the calends of January (Christmas holidays) those forbidden, ridiculous, ancient, and disreputable things, such as dancing, or keeping open house all night, or getting drunk. Let no one on the Feast of St. John, or any other saint, celebrate *solstices* by dances, carols, or diabolical chants."

In the provincial Council of York, in A. D. 1466, it was declared, with St. Thomas, that "all superstition was idolatry." "On the whole," continues Mr. Henderson, "it certainly appears that the early and mediæval Churches in their *collective* form, far from consciously encouraging heathenish superstition, constantly protested against it. Individual clergy in remote districts may have taken a different line, as St. Patrick is said to have done in engrafting Christianity on Paganism with so much skill, that he won over the people to the Christian religion before they understood the exact difference between the two systems of belief. At any rate — and jesting aside — the old superstition has lived on with marvelous vitality, and the Reformation, at least on the Continent, and in Scotland, has done little to check it. On the contrary, it would seem that the popular mind, when cut away from communion with the angelic world and saints departed, fastened the more readily upon a supernatural system of another order."

NOTE.—In Sweden, "on St. John's Eve, they gather and bind together all sorts of flowers and plants, which they call Midsommers-qvastar (Midsummer-posies). These are hung up in every house, particularly in the stables, the cattle then cannot be bewitched. The St. John's wort [hypericum] must be among the rest, as possessing extraordinary virtue. On St. John's Eve much may happen; and much be foreseen of importance for a person's remaining life." The love-sick entwines wreaths of nine sorts of flowers and lays them under his or her pillow, and whatever dreams "whisper over such flowers will prove true." — *Thorpe.*

CHAPTER XVIII.

HARVEST HOME.

MONG the ancient festivals the revival of which in our times has met with especial favor and acceptance is that of the old English Harvest Home. In its religious aspect, at least, this holiday corresponds with our National Thanksgiving. Indeed, the New England festival in all probability has been derived from that of old England, divested, of course, of "heathenish" ceremonies, for in the eyes of scrupulous Puritanism, such a custom as that depicted in our full page illustration must have seemed like a return to the idolatrous worship of Ceres.

As among the ancient Jews the feast of the " Harvest-Home " was identical with the Feast of Pentecost, and as the Whitsun festival is but a continuation of this most ancient of festivals, we have reserved the consideration of its poetical and picturesque observances for this the concluding chapter.

The Jewish festival of Pentecost, says Mr. Blunt, in his " Key to the Prayer-Book," is supposed to have been instituted by God as a memorial of the day on which he gave the Law to Moses, and declared the Israelites " a peculiar treasure, a kingdom of priests, and an holy nation " (Exodus xix. 5, 6): an object of the day which makes its connection with Whitsunday, the day when the Holy Ghost descended to sanctify a new Israel for " a peculiar people and a royal priesthood," very significant. But the prominent character of the day was that of a solemn harvest festival. Fifty days previously, the first cut sheaf of *corn* was offered to God for a blessing on the harvest then about to begin. On the day of Pentecost, two loaves of the first new *bread* were offered (with appointed burnt offerings) in thanksgiving for the harvest then ended; and this aspect of the feast has also a striking significance. For, as Christ was the " Corn of Wheat " which (having " fallen into the ground and died " on the day of the Passover) had borne much fruit when it sprung up a new and perpetual Sacrifice to God on Easter Day, so the five thousand baptized on the day of Pentecost were the first offering to God of the " One Bread " of the Lord's Body. (1 Cor. x. 17.)

Not only has this Feast of Ingathering or Harvest-Home, been observed under Jewish dispensations, but it seems also that wherever throughout the earth, especially among Christian nations, there is such a thing as a formal harvest, there also appears an inclination to mark it with a festive celebration.

This festival of Ingathering has been observed in England at a much later period of the year than that prescribed by the Law of Moses, for the obvious reason that the grain crops were not ripe for the sickle in England until the end of Summer or the beginning of Autumn.

Among our forefathers, St. Rock's Day (August 16) was generally celebrated as the Harvest-Home. The festival is now, however, observed on different days, and much later in the season. The late ripening of the Indian corn in this country, may, perhaps, account for the still later observance with us of the Harvest-Home or Thanksgiving. It is to be regretted, however, that our practice of deferring this festival of Ingathering to the end of November, although convenient in some respects, deprives us of the enjoyment of many of those picturesque rural customs and ceremonies which distinguish the Harvest-Home of our ancestors. The month of October, with its gorgeous display of autumnal leaves, fruits, and flowers, would seem much more appropriate, and would be more in harmony with the usages of other Christian nations. Says the "Book of Days"—

"Most of the old harvest customs were connected with the in-gathering of the crops, but some of them began with the commencement of harvest work. Thus in the southern counties of England, it was customary for the laborers to elect from among themselves a leader, whom they denominated their 'lord.' To him all the rest were required to give precedence, and to leave all transactions respecting their work. He made the terms with the farmers for mowing, for reaping, and for all the rest of the harvest work; he took the lead with the scythe, with the sickle, and on the 'carrying-days;' he was to be the first to eat, and the first to drink, at all their refreshments; his mandate was to be law to all the rest, who were bound to address him as 'My Lord,' and to show him all due honor and respect. Disobedience in any of these particulars was punished by imposing fines according to a scale previously agreed on by 'the lord' and all his vassals. In some instances, if any of his men swore or told a lie in his presence, a fine was inflicted. In Buckinghamshire and other counties 'a lady' was elected as well as 'a lord,' which often added much merriment to the harvest season. For while the lady was to receive all honors due to the lord from the rest of the laborers, he (for the lady was one of the workmen) was required to pass it on to the lord. For instance, at drinking time, the vassals were to give the horn first to the lady, who passed it to the lord, and when he had drunk, *she* drank next, and then the others indiscriminately. Every departure from this rule incurred a fine. The blunders which led to fines, of course, were frequent, and produced great merriment.

"In the old simple days of England, before the natural feelings of the people had been checked and chilled by Puritanism in the first place, and what may be called gross Commercialism in the second, the Harvest-Home was such a scene as Horace's friends might have expected to see at his Sabine farm, or as Theocritus described in his ' Idyls.' Perhaps it really was the very same scene which was presented in ancient times. The grain last cut was brought home in its wagon called the hock-cart, surmounted by a figure formed of a sheaf with gay dressings — a presumable representation of the goddess Ceres — while a pipe and tabor went merrily sounding in front, and the reapers tripped around· in a hand in hand ring, singing appropriate songs, or simply by shouts and cries giving vent to the excitement of the day.

> " ' Harvest-Home, Harvest-Home ;
> We have ploughed, we have sowed,
> We have reaped, we have mowed,
> We have brought home every load ;
> Hip, hip, hip, Harvest-Home ! '

" So they sang or shouted. In Lincolnshire and other districts, hand-bells were carried by those riding on the last load, and the following rhymes were sung : —

> " ' The boughs do shake, and the bells do ring,
> So merrily comes our harvest in,
> Our harvest in, our harvest in,
> So merrily comes our harvest in !
> Hurrah ! '

" Sometimes, the image on the cart, instead of being a mere dressed up bundle of grain, was a pretty girl of the reaping band, crowned with flowers, and hailed as *the maiden.* Of this we have a description in a ballad of Bloomfield's : —

> " ' Home came the jovial hockey load,
> Last of the whole year's crop,
> And Grace among the green boughs rode,
> Right plump upon the top.

> " ' This way and that the wagon reeled,
> And never queen rode higher ;

Her cheeks were colored in the field,
And ours before the fire.'

"In some provinces — for instance in Buckinghamshire — it was
a favorite practical joke to lay an ambuscade at some place where a
high bank or a tree gave opportunity, and drench the hock-cart
party with water.   Great was the merriment when this was cleverly
and effectively done, the riders laughing, while they shook themselves, as merrily as the rest.

"In the North of England, as the reapers went on during the last
day, they took care to leave a good handful of the grain uncut, but
laid down flat, and covered over; and when the field was done, the
'bonniest lass' was allowed to cut this final handful, which was
presently dressed up with various sewings, tyings, and trimmings,
like a doll, and hailed as a *corn baby.*   It was brought home in
triumph, with music of fiddlers and bagpipes, was set up conspicu-
ously that night at supper, and was usually preserved in the farmer's
parlor for the remainder of the year.   The bonny lass who cut this
handful of grain, was deemed the Har'st Queen."

In the ceremony described above, we are reminded
of the Scripture story of Ruth, that Harvest Queen of
other days.

The following examples, from the Rev. Edward
Cutts' "Book of Church Decoration," are selected in
illustration of the more modern usage in England,
where the *religious* aspect of the Feast of Ingathering,
seems to have been particularly revived: —

"At St. George's, Winkleigh, Devon, the church was reopened
after restoration, for the Harvest Festival, and the church. was
handsomely decorated.   For this purpose every farmer of the parish
was asked to give a sheaf of corn for the decoration of the
church, and what was not used for the purpose, would be distributed

to the poor. The farmers were unanimous in complying with the request, and many offered more than was asked for. The day was kept as a general holiday, and several triumphal arches adorned the village. The church was decorated with corn and flowers, the thank-offerings of the parishioners. Long lines of ears of wheat swept round the arches of the aisles, with hop-flowers twining gracefully up the granite pillars ; from the font, through the aisles to the chancel gleamed the golden grain, interspersed with flowers and mottoes.

"At All Saints', Lullingstone, Derbyshire, the parishioners went to church in procession, every one carrying a beautiful bouquet of geranium and wheat ears. On arriving at the church-yard gate, the band ceased playing ; the harvest hymn, which follows, was sung : —

> " 'Come, ye thankful people, come
> Raise the song of Harvest-Home !
> All is safely gathered in
> Ere the winter storms begin ;
> God, our Maker, doth provide
> For our wants to be supplied ;
> Come to God's own Temple, come ;
> Raise the song of Harvest-Home !'

and so singing, clergy, choir, and people, entered the church in order. Everything spoke of the harvest. On either side the porch rested a good sheaf of wheat. Wheat sheaves, with bunches of grapes, were laid upon the white-vested altar. Every standard in nave and aisles bore its selected ears of corn ; the flower-wreaths which crept round the stalls and lectern, were interlaced with the golden wheat ear. The font was surmounted with a canopy of flowers terminating in a tall floral cross.

At South Newton, Wilts, the parishioners went to church in procession ; first, banners and a band of music, then three men in their smock-frocks, bearing sheaves of wheat, oats, and barley ; then the Salisbury Plain Shepherds bearing their crooks, tied round with locks of wort and ribands ; then the farmers, and then the laborers, two by two.

"At Paulton, Somerset, over the church-yard gate, was a pretty
and tasteful design of flowers interspersed with corn and evergreens,
flanked by two small sheaves of corn, one of wheat and the other
of barley. Several flags floated in the breeze from the ancient
tower, and during the day the bells rung merry peals.

"At East Brent, also, a loaf of the New Year's corn was presented and used for the Holy Communion. At St. John's, Leicester,
the wreaths round the capitals and along the string courses, were of
plaited wheat, oats, barley, and ivy, with red berries and red and blue
flowers interspersed. In the decoration of the pulpit and font,
evergreens, corn, scarlet and blue flowers, fern, twigs of barberry
were used strung together with the branches of red barberries hanging down, and the effect is spoken of as being very successful. On
the communion table were laid a group of two sheaves of wheat,
with bunches of purple and white grapes, on a background of vine
leaves, between the sheaves; and on the wall behind, encircling an
I. H. S. of wheat ears, was a star of vine leaves, grapes, and
flowers, having worked within it, in grains of wheat, the text, 'I am
the Bread of Life.'"

In conclusion, we quote Herrick's felicitous description of the convivialities which attended the Harvest-
Home thanksgiving of the olden time: —

> "Come, sons of summer, by whose toile
> We are the Lords of wine and oile;
> By whose tough labours, and rough hands,
> We rip up first, then reap our lands,
> Crown'd with the ears of corne, now come,
> And to the pipe sing Harvest-Home.
> Come forth, my Lord, and see the cart,
> Drest up with all the country art.
> See here a maukin, there a sheet,
> As spotlesse pure as it is sweet;

The horses, mares, and frisking fillies,
Clad, all, in linnen white as lillies;
The harvest swaines and wenches bound
For joy, to see the hock-cart crown'd;
About the cart, heare how the rout
Of rural younglings raise the shout,
Pressing before, some coming after,
Those with a shout and these with laughter.
Some blesse the cart; some kiss the sheaves;
Some prank them up with oaken leaves;
Some crosse the fill-horse; some with great
Devotion stroak the home borne wheat:
While other rusticks, lesse attent
To prayers than to merryment
Run after with their breeches rent.
Well, on, brave boyes to your Lord's hearth
Glitt'ring with fire, where for your mirth
You shall see first the large and cheefe
Foundation of your feast, fat beefe;
With upper stories, mutton, veale,
And bacon, which makes full the meale;
With sev'rall dishes standing by,
As here a custard, there a pie,
And here all tempting frumentie.
And for to make the merrie cheere
If smirking wine be wanting here,
There's that which drowns all care, stout beere,
Which freely drink to your Lord's health,
Then to the plough, the commonwealth;
Next to your flailes, your fanes, your fatts,
Then to the maids with wheaten hats;
To the rough sickle, and the crookt sythe
Drink, frollick, boyes, till all be blythe,
Feed and grow fat, and as ye eat,

Be mindfull that the lab'ring neat,
As you, may have their full of meat ;
And know, besides, you must revoke
The patient oxe unto the yoke,
All, all goe. back unto the plough
And harrow, though they're hang'd up now.
And you must know, your Lord's word 's true,
"Feed him you must, whose food fills you."
And that the pleasure is like rain,
Not sent you for to drowne your paine ;
But for to make it spring againe."

In Excelsis Gloria.

GERMAN CAROL. Tune, 16th Century.

1. When Christ was born of Ma - ry
2. The Shep - herds saw the an - gels

Dim.

free In Beth - le - hem that fair ci -
bright, They shone with such a heav'n - ly

tie, An - gels sang with mirth and glee
light, "O God's denr son is born to - night,"

In ex - cel - sis Glo - ri - a   An - gels
In ex - cel sis Glo - ri - a " " O God's dear

sang with mirth and glee, In ex - cel - sis
son is born to - night," In ex - cel - sis

glo - ri - a   In ex - cel - sis
glo - ri - a   In ex - cel - sis

glo - ri - a   glo - - - - ri - - - - a.
glo - ri - a   glo - - - - ri - - - - a.

Christmas Day in the Morning.

TRADITIONAL. (Kent.)

I saw three ships come sail - ing in, On
Christ - mas day, on Christ - mas day; I saw three ships come
sail - ing in, On Christ - mas day in the morn - ing.

* For remaining verses, see Chapter III., page 24.

As Joseph was a Walking.

TRADITIONAL. (Somersetshire.)

p As Jo - seph was a walk - ing, He heard an an - gel sing, This night shall be the birth - time Of Christ the heav'n-ly King.

* For remaining verses, see Chapter III., page 19.

The Holy Well.

TRADITIONAL (Derbyshire).

As it fell out one May morn-ing, And on a bright holi-

day, Sweet Je-sus asked of his dear mother, If he might go to

play, "To play, to play, sweet Jesus shall go, And to play now get you

gone, And let me hear of no complaint, At night when you come home.

For remaining verses, see Chap. III., page 20.

The Holly and the Ivy.

OLD FRENCH CAROL TUNE.

The Hol - ly and the Ivy, Now both are full well grown; Of all the trees that spring in wood, The Hol - ly bears the crown. The

CHORUS.

The

For remaining verses, see Chap. III., page 26.

Hol - ly bears a blos - som as white as a lily
ris - ing of the sun, The *running of the*

flow'r ; and Ma - ry bore sweet Je - sus Christ To
deer, The *play-ing of the or - gan,* The

be our sweet Sa - viour, To be our sweet Sa - viour.
singing in the choir, The *singing in the choir.*

The Boars-head Carol.

Arranged by E. F. Rimbault, LL. D.

TREBLE SOLO.
Slow and majestic.

1. The Boar's head in hand bear I, Be-
2. The Boar's head, as I un - der- stand, Is the
3. Our stew - ard hath pro - vi - ded this In

Accomp.

rall. *a tempo.*

decked with bays and rose- ma- ry; And I pray you, my mas- ters
brav - est dish in all the land ; when thus be - decked with
hon - or of the King of Bliss; Which on this day to be

be mer - ry, *Quot es - tis in con - vi - vi - o.*
gay gar - land, Let us *Ser - ve - re can - ti - co.*
serv - ed is *In Re - gi - men - si a - tri - o.*

CHORUS.

TREBLE.

Ca - put a - pri de - fe - ro, Red - dens laud - es do - mi - no.

ALTO.

Ca - put a - pri de - fe - ro, Red - dens laud - es do - mi - no.

TENOR. (8ve lower.)

Ca - put a - pri de - fe - ro, Red - dens laud - es do - mi - no.

BASS.

Ca - put a - pri de - fe - ro, Red - dens laud - es do - mi - no.

CHO.
ACCOMP.

Ca - put a - pri de - fe - ro, Red - dens laud - es do - mi - no.

APPENDIX.

CHRISTMAS PLAYS.

The old Christmas play of "St. George and the Dragon," says Mr. Hervey, is still amongst the most popular amusements of this season, in many parts of England. The Guisards in Scotland also perform a play which is of similar construction, and evidently borrowed from the same source. Sir Walter Scott, in his notes to "Marmion," speaks of this play, as one in which he and his companions were in the habit of taking parts when boys; and mentions the characters of the old Scripture plays having got mixed up with it in the version familiar to him. He enumerates St. Peter, who carried the keys, St. Paul, who was armed with a sword, and Judas, who had the bag for contributions; and says that he believes there was also a St. George. The confusion of characters, in all the different versions, is very great. In the Whitehaven edition given below, Saint or Prince George is son to the king of Egypt and the hero who carried all before him is Alexander. The characters in the play of St. George and the Dragon, given by Hervey, are — The Turkish Knight, Father Christmas, The King of Egypt, Saint George, The Dragon, and Giant Turpin.

The same play with slight variations is also to be found in Sandys' "Christmas Tide;" but as the most amusing of these Christmas Plays is that of Alexander and the King of Egypt, mentioned above, it is here subjoined as a specimen.

ALEXANDER, OR THE KING OF EGYPT.

A MOCK PLAY, AS IT IS ACTED BY THE MUMMERS EVERY CHRISTMAS.

Act I. — Scene I.

Enter ALEXANDER.

ALEXANDER.

SILENCE, brave gentlemen. If you will give an eye,
Alexander is my name, I'll sing a tragedy.
A ramble here I took, the country for to see,
Three actors I have brought so far from Italy ;
The first I do present, he is a noble king,
He 's just come from the wars — good tidings he doth bring.
The next that doth come in, he is a doctor good,
Had it not been for him I'd surely lost my blood.
Old Dives is the next, a miser, you may see,
Who, by lending of his gold, is come to poverty.
So, gentlemen, you see our actors will go round ;
Stand off a little while — more pastime will be found.

Act I. — Scene II.

Enter ACTORS.

Room, room, brave gallants — give us room to sport,
For in this room we wish for to resort —
Resort, and to repeat to you our merry rhyme ;
For remember, good sirs, this is Christmas time.
The time to cut up goose-pies now doth appear,
So we are come to act our merry Christmas here ;
At the sound of the trumpet and beat of the drum,
Make room, brave gentlemen, and let our actors come ;
We are the merry actors that traverse the street,
We are the merry actors that fight for our meat ;

We are the merry actors that show pleasant play,
Step in, thou King of Egypt, and clear the way.

KING OF EGYPT.

I am the King of Egypt, as plainly doth appear,
And Prince George he is my only son and heir.
Step in, therefore, my son, and act thy part with me,
And show forth thy fame before the company.

PRINCE GEORGE.

I am Prince George, a champion *brave* and *bold*,
For with my spear I've won three crowns of gold.
'Twas I that brought the dragon to the slaughter,
And I that gained th' Egyptian Monarch's daughter.
In Egypt's fields I prisoner long was kept,
But by my valor I from them escaped :
I sounded loud at the gate of a divine,
And out came a giant of no good design ;
He gave me a blow which almost struck me dead,
But I up with my sword, and cut off his head.

ALEXANDER.

Hold, slasher, hold ! pray do not be so hot,
For in this spot thou knowest not who thou'st got ;
'Tis I that's to hash thee and smash thee as small as flies,
And send thee to Satan,[1] to make mince pies.
Mince pies hot, mince pies cold —
I'll send thee to Satan ere thou'rt three days old.
But hold ! Prince George, before you go away,
Either you or I must die this bloody day ;
Some mortal wounds thou shalt receive of me —
So let us fight it out most manfully.

[1] In another version it is "to Jamaica."

Act II. — Scene I.

ALEXANDER *and* PRINCE GEORGE *fight — The Latter is wounded and falls.*

KING OF EGYPT.

Curst Christian! what is this thou hast done?
Thou hast ruined me by killing my best son.

ALEXANDER.

He gave me a challenge.   How should I him deny?
And see how low he lies who was so high.

KING OF EGYPT.

O, Sambo, Sambo, help me now,
For I was never more in need,
For thee to stand with sword in hand,
And to fight at my command.

DOCTOR.

Yes, my liege, I will thee obey,
And by my sword I hope to win the day:
Yonder stands he who has killed my master's son,
And has his ruin thoughtlessly begun;
I'll try if he be sprung from Royal blood,
And through his body make an ocean flood.
Gentlemen, you see my sword's point is broke,
Or else I'd run it through that villain's throat.

KING OF EGYPT.

Is there never a doctor to be found
That can cure my son of his deadly wound?

DOCTOR.

Yes, there is a doctor to be found
That can cure your son of his deadly wound.

KING OF · EGYPT.

What diseases can he cure?

DOCTOR.

All sorts of diseases,
Whatever you pleases —
The phthisic, the palsy, and gout —
If the devil were in, I'd blow him out.

KING OF EGYPT.

What is your fee?

DOCTOR.

Fifteen pounds is my fee,
 The money to lay down;
But as 'tis such an one as he,
 I'll cure him for ten pound.
I carry a little bottle of alicumpane;
 Here, Jack, take a little of my flip-flop,
 Pour it down thy lip-top,
Rise up and fight again.

> [*The Doctor performs his cure as the scene closes.*

Act III. — Scene II.

PRINCE GEORGE (*arises*).

O, horrible, terrible! the like was never seen —
A man drove out of seven senses into fifteen,
And out of fifteen into fourscore —
O, horrible! O, terrible! the like was ne'er before.

ALEXANDER.

Thou silly ass, thou liv'st on grass;
 Dost thou abuse a stranger?
I live in hopes to buy new ropes
 And tie thy nose to a manger.

PRINCE GEORGE.

Sir, unto you I give my hand.

ALEXANDER.

Stand off, thou slave! Think thee not my friend!

PRINCE GEORGE.

A slave, sir! That's for me far too base a name —
That word deserves to stab thine honor's fame.

ALEXANDER.

To be stabbed, sir, is least of all my care —
Appoint your time and place, I'll meet you there.

PRINCE GEORGE.

I'll cross the water at the hour of five.

ALEXANDER.

I'll meet you there, sir, if I be alive!

PRINCE GEORGE.

But stop, sir, I'll wish you a wife, both lusty and young,
Can talk Dutch, French, and th' Italian tongue.

ALEXANDER.

I'll have none such!

PRINCE GEORGE.

Why? Don't you love your learning?

ALEXANDER.

Yes; I love my learning, as I love my life;
I love a learned scholar, but not a learned wife.
        Stand off, etc. (*as before*).

KING OF EGYPT.

Sir, to express thy beauty I'm not able,
For thy face shines as the kitchen table;
Thy teeth are no whiter than the charcoal, etc.

ALEXANDER.

Stand off, thou dirty dog, or by my sword thou'lt die —
I'll make thy body full of holes, and cause thy buttons fly.

Act IV. — Scene I.

KING OF EGYPT *fights and is killed.*

Enter PRINCE GEORGE.

O, what is here ?   O, what is to be done ?
Our King is slain — the crown is likewise gone.
Take up his body, bear it hence away,
For in this place it shall no longer stay.

CONCLUSION.

Bouncer !   Buckler !   Velvet 's dear,
And Christmas comes but once a year,
Though when it comes it brings good cheer.
But farewell, Christmas, once a year —
Farewell — farewell — adieu friendship and unity,
I hope we have made sport and pleased the company.
But, gentlemen, you see we're but actors four,
We've done our best — and the best can do no more.[1]

---

[1] "These tragic performers wear white trowsers and waistcoats, showing their shirt-sleeves, and are much decorated with ribbons and handkerchiefs — each carrying a drawn sword in his hand, if they can be procured, otherwise a cudgel. They wear high caps of pasteboard, covered with fancy paper, adorned with beads, small pieces of looking-glass, bugles, etc. — several long strips of different colored cloth strung on them, the whole having a fanciful and smart effect.   The Doctor, who is a sort of merry-andrew to the piece, is dressed in some ridiculous way, with a three-cornered hat and painted face."

"The Turk sometimes has a turban ; Father Christmas is personified as a grotesque old man, wearing a large mask and wig, with a huge club in his hand.   The female, when there is one, is in the costume of her great-grandmother.   The hobby-horse, when introduced, has a sort of representation of a horse's hide, but the dragon and the giant, when there is one, frequently appear with the same style of dress as the knights."

"NORTHUMBERLAND HOUSEHOLD BOOK."

The following curious Items from the Northumberland House-hold Book of Earl Percy, 1512, together with the Inventory of the splendid Robes of Office and ornaments of a Barne or Boy Bishop,[1] taken from an ancient MS., is abridged from the "Antiquarian Repertory."

"Item. My Lord usith and accustomyth yerely when his Lord-ship is at home to yef unto the Barne Bishop of Beverley when he comith to my Lorde in Cristmas Holly Dayes when my Lord kepith his Hous at Lokynfèld — xx⁸.

"Item. My Lorde useth and accustomyth to gif yerely when his Lordship is at home to the Barne-Bishop of Yorke when he comes over to my Lord in Cristynmase Holly Dayes as he is accustomede yerely — xx⁸.

"Item. My Lord useth and accustomth to gyfe yerely upon Saynt Nicolas — Even if he kepe chapell for Saynt Nicolas to the Master of his children of his chapell for one of the children of his chapell yerely vi.⁸ viij.ᵈ And if Saynt Nicolas com owt of the Towne wher my Lord lyeth and my Lord kepe no chapell than to hove yerely iii.⁸ iiij.ᵈ — vi.⁸ viij.ᵈ

"Item. My Lord useth and accustomyth to gyfe yerely if his Lord-ship kepe a Chapell and be at home, them of his Lordschipes Chapell if they do play the play of the Nativite uppon Cristenmes day in the mornnynge in my Lords Chapell befor his Lordship — xx.⁸

---

[1] In Hearne's "Liber Niger Scaccarii, 1728," we find that Archbishop Ro-theram bequeathed "a myter for the Barne bishop, of cloth of gold, with two knopps of silver gilt and enamyled." In Lysons's "Environs of London," among his curious extracts from the Church-warden's Accounts at Lambeth, is the follow-ing: "1523. For the Bishop's dynner and hys company on St. Nycolas Day, ijs. viijd." The Church-warden's Accounts of St. Mary-at-Hill, London, 10 Henry VI., mention two children's copes, also a myter of cloth of gold set with stones." Under 1549, also, Lucas and Stephen, church-wardens, is : "For 12 oz. silver, being clasps of books and the bishop's mitre, at vs. viijd. per oz. vjl. xvjs. jd." These last were sold. In the "Inventory of Church Goods," belonging to the same parish, at the same time, we have : "Item, a mitre for a Bishop at St. Nicholas-tyde, garnished with silver and amelyd, and perle, and counterfeit stone."   16

"Item. My Lorde useth and accustomyth to gyf yerely when his Lordschippe is home and hath an Abbot of Miserewll (Misrule) in Cristynmas in his Lordschippis House uppon New-Yers-day in reward — xx.ˢ

"Item. My Lorde useth and accustomyth yerly to gyf hym which is ordyned to be Master of the Revells yerly in my Lords House in Cristmas for the overseyinge and orderinge of his Lordships Plays, Interludes and Dresinge that is plaid befor his Lordship in his House in the xij^{th} Dayes of the Cristenmas and they to have in rewarde for that caus yerly — xxˢ."

The following is an Inventory of the splendid robes and ornaments belonging to a Barne or Boy-Bishop, taken from an ancient MS.

Contenta De Ornamentis Epi. Puer.

(E Rotulo in pergamen.)

"Imprimis. i Myter well garnished with Perle and precious Stones, with Nowches of Silver and Gilt before and behind.

"Item. iiij Rynges of Silver and Gilt, with four ridde Precious Stones in them.

"Item i Pontifical with Silver and Gilt, with a blue Stone in hytt.

"It. i Owche broken Silver and Gilt, with iiij Precious Stones and a Perle in the mydds.

"It. A Croose, with a Staff of Coper and Gilt, with the Ymage of St Nicolas in the mydds.

"It. i Vestment redde with Lyons, with Silver, with Brydds of Gold in the Orferes of the same.·

"It. i Albe to the same with Starres in the paro.

"Item. i White Cope, stayned with Tristells and Orferes redde Sylke with Does of Gold and whytt Napkins about the Necks.

"It. iiij Copes blew Sylk with red Orferes trayled with whitt Braunchis and Flowres.

"It. i Steyned Cloth of the Ymage of St Nicholas.

"It. i Tabard of Skarlet and a Hodde thereto, lyned with whitt Sylk.

"It. A Hode of Skarlett lyned with blue Sylk."

The Lord Abbot of misrule, mentioned above, appears to have been the same popular character that was known after the Reformation (when the term Abbot had acquired an ill sound) by the title Lord of Misrule. The Scottish Abbot of Un-reason was also, it seems, identical in many particulars, with the English Abbot of Misrule. Sir Walter Scott has given a spirited description of the proceedings of this mock prelate in "The Abbot," vol. i., chap. xiv. In Scotland, where the Reformation took a more severe and gloomy turn, this and some other sportive characters were thought worthy an Act of Parliament to suppress them. See the 6th Parlia. of Queen Mary of Scotland, 1555.

"Item. It is Statute and ordained that in all times cumming na maner of persons be chosen ' Robert Hude ' nor ' Little John ' ' Abbot of Un-reason ' ' Queenis of May' nor utherwise nouther in Burgh nor in Landwart (*i. e.* in the Country) in onie times to cum." And this under very high penalty, viz., " to the chusers of such characters loss of freedom and other punishment at the Queen's Grace' Will " and banishment from the realme to the " acceptor of sic-like office."

NOTE 1. — " The well-known festivity of the Eton-Montem, abolished in 1847, appears to have originated in and been a continuance under another form of the mediæval custom of the Boy-Bishop. In recent times, this Eton-Montem festival used to be celebrated on Whitsun Tuesday, but previous to 1759, it took place on the first Tuesday in Hilary Term, which commences on 23d January. At a still remoter period, the celebration appears to have been held about the Christmas Holidays, on one of the days between the feasts of St. Nicholas and the Holy Innocents. One of the customs, certainly a relic of the Boy-Bishop revels, was after the procession reached Salt Hill ('Ad Montem,' whence the name of the festival) for a boy habited in clerical vestments, to read prayers, whilst another officiated as a clerk, who at the conclusion of the service was kicked down hill by the parson. This irreverent part of the ceremonies however was latterly abrogated, in deference to the wishes of Queen Charlotte."

NOTE 2. — Among the popular dramatic exhibitions, similar in some respects to those above noticed, which even so late as the beginning of the reign of Queen Elizabeth, were enacted in many of the principal churches in England, was that of the Sepulchre Show, or Watching the Holy Sepulchre at Easter, the subject of the representation being taken from the Gospel for the Day.

The custom was to erect in the church a representation of the sepulchre, and the consecrated wafer being placed in it on the Eve of the Festival remained until the Morning of Easter Day.

In an old Parish Record there is an entry of one Roger Brook, playing the part of watchman on such an occasion, for which he was paid eight-pence, and a note is appended to the account, stating that this was a ceremony used in churches in remembrance of the soldiers watching the Sepulchre of Our Saviour.

Mr. Fosbrooke gives the "properties" of the Sepulchre-show belonging to St. Mary Redcliffe's Church at Bristol, from an original manuscript in his possession formerly belonging to Chatterton : — "Master Cannings hath delivered the . 4th day of July in the year of Our Lord 1470 to Master Nicholas Pelles Vicar of Redcliffe, Moses Conterin, Philip Barthelmew, and John Brown, procurators of Redcliffe beforesaid, a new sepulchre well guilt with fine gold and a civer thereto ; an image of God Almighty rising out of the same sepulchre, with all the ordinance that longeth thereto ; that is to say, a lath made of timber and iron work thereto. Item, Hereto longeth Heaven made of timber and stained cloths. Item, Hell made of timber and iron work thereto, with Devils, the number of Thirteen. Item, Four Knights armed, keeping the Sepulchre, with their weapons in their hands ; that is to say, two spears, two axes, with two shields. Item, Four pair of angels wings for four angels, made of timber and well painted. Item, the Fadre, the crown and visage, the *ball* with a cross upon it well guilt with fine gold. Item, the Holy Ghost coming out of heaven into the Sepulchre. Item, longeth to the four angels four Perukes."

"It hapned in the yeare of our Lord 1607 the 31 of October
beinge All Sayntes Eue, that at night a fier was made in the Hall
of St. John Baptist's Colledge in Oxon, accordinge to the custome
and statuts of the same place, at wch time the whole companye or
the most parte of the Students of the same house mette toogether
to beginne their Christmas, of wch some came to see sports, to witte
the Seniors as well Graduates, as Vnder-graduates. Others to make
sports, viz. Studentes of the second yeare, whom they call Poulderlings, others to make sporte wth all, of this last sort were they
whome they call Fresh-menn . . . . But (as it often falleth out)
the Freshmen patients, thinkinge the Poulderlings or Agentes too
buysie and nimble, They them too dull and backwarde in theyr
duety, the standers by findinge both of them too forwarde & vio-
lente, the sports for that night for fear of tumultes weare broken vpp,
euerye mann betakinge himselfe to his reste. The next night followinge, beinge the feast of All Sayntes, at nighte they mett agayne
together ; And thereas yt was hoped a nights sleepe would haue
somewhat abated theyr rage, it contraryewise set a greater edge on
theyr furye, they hauinge all this while but consulted how to gett
more strength on agaynst another, and consequently to breed newe
quarrells and contradictions, in so much that the strife and conten-
tions of youthes & children had like to haue sett Men together
by the eares, to the vtter annihalatinge of all Christmas sportes for
the whole yeare followinge. Wherefore for the auoydinge both the
one, and the other, some who studied the quiet of all, mentioned
the choosinge of a Christmas Lord, or Prince of the Revells, who
should have authorytie both to appoynt & moderate all such games,

and pastimes as should ensue & to punishe all offenders wch should any way hinder or interrupte the free & quiet passage of any auntient & allowed sporte.

" This motion (for that the person of a Prince or Lorde of the Revells had not biñe knowen amongst them for thirty yeares . . . .) was p'sentlye allowed and greedilye apprehended of all ; Wher vpon 13 of the senior Vnder graduates, ... wth drew themselues into the parlor, where after longe debatinge whether they should chouse a Graduate or an Vnder Graduate, thinkinge the former would not vouchsafe or vndertake yt at theyr appoyntmentes, ye latter should not be vpheld & backed as yt was meete & necessary for such a place, they came forth rather to make triall what should be doñe, than to resolue what should be doñe. And therefore at their first entrance into the Hall meeting Sr Towse a younge mañ (as they thought) fitt for the choyse, they layed handes on him, and by maine strength liftinge him vpp, viua voce, pronounced him Lord. But hee as strongelye refusinge the place as they violentlye thrust it vpon him, shewinge wth all, reasons why hee could by no meanes vndergoe suc a charge, they gott onlye this good by their first attempt, that they vnderstood heer by how that ye whole Colledge was rather willinge a Senior Batchelour at least, yf not a junior M^r should be chosen into the place rather than any Vnder graduate, because they would rather an earnest sporte than a scoffinge jest should be made of it. Wher fore the Electors retourninge againe into the Parlor and shuttinge the dore close vpon themselves beganne more seriously to consult of the matter, and findinge some vnable, some vnwillinge to take the place, at length they concluded to make the 2 assay but wth more formalitie and deliberation ; resoluinge yf they were not now seconded of all handes, to meddle no more wth it. Wherfore entringe ye second time into the Hall they desired one of the 10 Seniors & one of the Deanes of the Colledge to hould Scrutinye and the Vice-Præsidcnt to sitt by as ouer-seer, who willingly harkninge to their request sate all 3 down at the highe Table : Then the Electors went vp one by one in senioritye to giue their voyce by writinge. . . . . At length all the voyces beinge giuen . . . . the Vice-Præsident wth the rest stoode vpp, and out of the abstract the Deane read distinctly in the hearinge of all p'sent as followeth

Nominantur in hoc Scrutinio duo quorum

{ 1us Joanes Towse, habet suffragia sex.

{ 2° Thomas Tucker, habet suffragia septem.

These wordes were not out of his mouthe before a generall and loud crie was made of Tucker, Tucker, Viuat, Viuat, &^{ct}. After wch all the younger sorte rañe forth of the Colledge, crieinge the same in the streets; wch Sr Tucker beinge then howsde not farr from the Colledge, ouer hearinge, kept himself close till the companye were past, and then, as soone and secretly as he could, gott him to his Chamber ; where (after he had biñe longe sought for abroad in the Towne, and at home in ye Colledge, haste and desire out runñinge it self, and seekinge there last where it might first finde) he was in mañer surprised, and more by violence than any will of his owne, taken vpp & with continuall & joyfull outcries, carried about ye Hall, and so back to his Chamber, as his owne request was, where for y^t night he rested, dismissinge ye Company and desiringe some time to thinke of their loues and goodwill and to consider of his owne charge and place."

[After a council held in the Hall of the College on the 5th of November, a subscription was determined upon, or rather "an auncient Act for taxes and subsidyes" made in 1577, in the reign of a preceding Christmas Prince was newly ratified and published.] It was enacted : —

"that no mañ dissemble his estate, or hide his abilitye, but be willinge at all times to pay such duetyes, taxes, and subsidies as shall be lawfully demaunded & thought reasonable "

[The subscription was headed by the College " Domus vi^{li} xiii iiii^d " Among the long list that follows appear the names of Laud and Juxon, both of them afterwards Archbishops of Canterbury.

The supply thus obtained, being found insufficient, a writ was served in due form to those who had been sometime Fellows or Commoners of the College.]

"Trusty and welbeloued wee greet you well. Allthough there bee nothinge more against our minde then to be drawne into any course that may burden our loyall Subjects, Yet such is our estate, at this time in regard of ye great and vrgent occasions fallinge and growinge dayly vpon vs without time or respiration as wee shalbe forced præsently to disburse greater soffies of money then is possible for vs to prouide by any ordinarye meanes, or to want wth out great præjudice. Sejng as well ye fame of our kingdome in ye entertayn-ment of forraine Princes & Embassadours, as ye safetie of our own person, and ye whole Coffionwealth, for the præuentinge of warrs and tumultes, likely to ensue, consisteth in ye wealth of our coffers as much as in any one meanes whatsoeuer. In which consideration wee think it needlesse to vse any more argumentes from such a Prince to such a Subject, but y^t, as our necessitie is ye only cause of our request, so your loue & duety must be ye cheife motiue of your ready perfourmance and helpe in furnishinge these our wantes, not only wth your person, but wth your purse in your owne absence : A matter wherof we make no doubt, beinge fully perswaded of your seruice and fidelitie. Therfore our will and pleasure is that præsently upon ye receipt hereof you cause a soffie of money ac-cording to y^r abilitie & greatnesse of y^r loue to bee deliuered to Thomas Clarke whom we haue appointed to be our Collector in ye County of Middlesex ; the lone whereof only we desire to be vntill ye next great yeare of Plato, then to be jmediatly repayd by vs or our successors to you or y^r Assignes y^t shall then demaund it.

"Giuen vnder our priuye Seale at our Pallace of St. Iohns in Oxen, the seuenth of December in the first yeare of our rayne, 1607."

. . . .

"For all these Subsidies at home, and helpes abroad, yet it was founde y^t in ye ende there would rather be want (as indeed it hap-ned) then any superfluitye, and therefore ye Prince tooke order wth the Bowsers to send out warrantes to all ye Tenantes & other

frendes of ye Colledge y^t they should send in extraordinary pro·
uision against euery Feast, wch accordingly was perfourmed ; Some
sendinge Money, some Wine, some Venison some other prouision,
euery one according to his abilitye.

" All things beinge thus sufficiently [as it was thought] prouided
for, ye Councell table wth ye Lord himself, mett together to nominate
Officers & to appoynt the day of ye Princes publike installment.
. . . . It was thought fitt that his [the Prince's] whole ensuinge
Regiment (for good lucke sake) should be consecrated to ye Deitie
of Fortune, as ye sole Mistres & Patronesse of his estate, and
therefore a schollarlike deuise called, Ara Fortunæ was prouided for
his installment. . . . . On St Thomas day at night ye officers before elect were solemnly proclaimed by a Sergeant at armes, and an
Herauld, ye trompetts soundinge beetwixt euery title. This Proclamation after it was read, was for a time hunge vp in ye Hall, y^t
euery mañ might ye better vnderstande ye qualitie of his owne place,
and they y^t were of lower, or no place, might learne what duety to
perfourme to others.

" The mañer whereof was as followeth :

" . . . . Therefore by these præsentes bee it knowne vnto all of
what estate or condicion soeuer whome it shall concerne y^t Thomas
Tucker an honorable wise & learned Gentlemen to ye great come-
forte of ye weale-publique from hence-forth to be reputed, taken and
obayed for the true, onely and vndoubted Monarche of this reuell-
linge Climate, whome ye generall consent and ioynte approbation
of ye whole Coffionwealth hath inuested and crowned with these
honours & titles followinge :

" The most magnificent and renowned *Thomas* by the fauour of
Fortune, Prince of Alba Fortunata, Lord St Iohns, high Regent of
ye Hall, Duke of St Giles, Marquesse of Magdalens Landgraue
of ye Groue, County Palatine of ye Cloisters, Cheife Bailiffe of y^e
Beaumonts, high Ruler of Rome, Maister of the Mañor of Wal-
tham, Gouernour of Gloster-green, sole Coffiaunder of all Tilts,
Tourneaments, and Triumphes, Superintendent in all Solemnities
whatsoeuer."

(Then comes the appointment of a long list of subordinate officers and deputies.)

From this time forward, and not before, the Prince was thought "fully to be enstalde, and y⁰ forme of gouernement fully established, in-so-much that none might or durst contradicte any thinge wᶜʰ was appoynted by himself, or any of his Officers."

In the " Miscellanea Antiqua Anglicana," from which the above is abridged, there is a lengthy account of the masks and entertainments which followed, written by an eye witness of, and performer in, the sports, printed for the first time (1815) from the original manuscript in the College Library.

THE LONDON MIDSUMMER HOLIDAYS.

(From Stow's Survey.)

" In the months of June and July, on the vigils of festival days and on the same festival days in the evenings after the sun setting there were usually made bonfires in the streets, every man bestowing wood or labour toward them ; the wealthier sort also, before their doors near to the said bonfires, would set out tables on the vigils, furnished with sweet bread and good drink, and on the festival days with meats and drinks plentifully, whereunto they would invite their neighbours and passengers also to sit and be merry with them in great familiarity, praising God for his benefits bestowed on them. These were called bonfires as well of good amity amongst neighbours that being before at controversy, were there, by the labour of others, reconciled, and made of bitter enemies loving friends ; and also for the virtue that a great fire hath to purge the infection of the air. On the vigil of St. John the Baptist, and on St. Peter and Paul the Apostles, every man's door being shadowed with green birch, long fennel, St. John's wort, orpin, white lilies, and such like, garnished upon with garlands of beautiful flowers, had also lamps of glass, with oil burning in them all the night ; some hung out branches of iron curiously wrought, containing hundreds of lamps alight at once, which made a goodly show, namely, in New Fish Street, Thames Street, etc. Then had ye besides the standing watches all in bright harness, in every ward and street of this city and suburbs a marching watch, that passed through the principal streets thereof, to wit, from the little conduit by Paule's Gate to West Cheap, by the stocks through Cornhill, by Leaden Hall to Aldgate, then back down through Fenchurch Street by Grasse Church, about Grasse Church conduit, and up Grasse Church Street into Cornhill, and through it into West Cheape again. The whole way for this marching watch extendeth to three thousand two hundred tailor's yards of assize ; for the furniture whereof with lights, there were appointed seven hundred cressets, five hundred of them being found by the companies, the other two hundred by the chamber of London. Besides the which lights every constable in London, in number more than two hundred and forty, had his cresset: the charge of every cresset was in light two shillings and fourpence, and every cresset had two men, one to bear or hold it, another to bear a bag with light and to serve it, so that the poor men pertaining to the cressets, taking wages, besides that every one had a straw hat, with a badge painted, and his breakfast in the morning, amounted in number to almost two thousand. The marching watch contained in number about two thousand men, part of them being old soldiers of skill, to be captains, lieutenants, sergeants, corporals, etc., wiflers, drummers and fifers, standard and ensign bearers, sword-players, trumpeters on horseback, demilances on great horses, gunners with hand guns, or half hakes, archers in coats of white fustian, signed on the breast and back with the arms of the city, their bows bent in their hands, with sheaves of arrows by their sides, pikemen in bright corslets, burganets, etc., halberds, the like billmen in almaine rivets, and apernes of mail in great number ; there were also divers pageants, morris-dancers, constables, the one-half, which was one hundred and twenty, on St. John's Eve, the other half on St. Peter's Eve in bright harness, some overgilt, and every one a jarnet of scarlet thereupon, and a chain of gold, his henchman following him, his minstrels before him, and his cresset light passing by him, the waits of the city, the mayor's officers for his guard before him, all in a livery of worsted, or say jackets parti-coloured, the mayor himself well mounted on horseback, the sword-bearer before him in fair armour, well mounted also, the mayor's footmen, and the like torch-bearers about him, henchmen twain upon great stirring horses, following him. The sheriff's watches came one after the other in like order, but not so large in number as the mayor's ; for where the mayor had besides his giant three pageants, each of the sheriffs had besides their giants but two pageants, each their morris-dance, and one henchman, their officers in jackets of worsted, or say parti-coloured, differing from the mayor's, and each from other, but having harnessed men a great many, etc.

"This midsummer watch was thus accustomed yearly, time out of mind, until the year 1539, the thirty-first of Henry VIII., in which year, on the 8th of May, a great muster was made by the citizens at the Mile's end, all in bright harness, with coats of white silk, or cloth and chains of gold, in three great battles, to the number of fifteen thousand, which passed through London to Westminster, and so through the sanctuary, and round about the park of St. James, and returned home through Oldborne. King Henry, then considering the great charges of the citizens for the furniture of this unusual muster, forbade the marching watch provided for at midsummer for that year, which being once laid down, was not raised again till the year 1548, the second of Edward VI., Sir John Gresham then being mayor, who caused the marching watch, both on the Eve of St. John the Baptist, and of St. Peter the apostle, to be revived and set forth in as comely order as it had been accustomed. Since this mayor's time the like marching watch in this city hath not been used, though some attempts have been made thereunto."

An ancient custom in connection with the above is also noticed by Stow, who says that the following custom was maintained in St. Paul's Cathedral on the Festival of St. Peter and St. Paul, which custom originated in an obligation incurred by Sir William Baud, in 1274 (in the third year of Edward I.), when he was permitted to enclose twenty acres of the Dean's land, in consideration of presenting the clergy of the cathedral with a fat buck and doe yearly on the days of the Conversion and Commemoration of St. Paul (25th of January and 29th of June). Stow says :—

"Now what I have heard by Report and have partly seen, it followeth. On the feast day of the commemoration of St. Paul, the buck being brought up to the steps of the high altar in St. Paul's Church, at the hour of procession the dean and chapter being apparelled in copes and vestments, with garlands of roses on their heads, they sent the body of the buck to baking, and had the head fixed on a pole, borne before the cross in their procession, until they issued out of the west door, where the keeper that brought it blowed the death of the buck, and then the horners that were about the city presently answered him in like manner ; for the which pains they had each one of the dean and chapter, fourpence in money, and their dinner, and the keeper that brought it was allowed during his abode there, for that service, meat, drink, and lodging, at the dean and chapter's charges, and five shillings in money at his going away, together with a loaf of bread, having the picture of St. Paul upon it, etc.

[There was belonging to the church of St. Paul, for both the days, two special suits of vestments, the one embroidered with bucks, the other with does, both given by the said Baud (as I have heard)."

["Stow was but an indifferent scholar himself; but then he having had the use of Mr. Leland's Notes (which are now lost), there are many excellent things in the work, and some of them learned and worthy the observation of even our best scholars." Thomas Hearne, exon. July 11, 1714.]

THE KIRMSE, OR KIRCH–MESSE.

(THE "CHURCH ALES" OF THURINGEN, SAXONY.)

ONE of the most important of the national festivals of Thuringian Saxony is that of Kirmse or Kirch-Messe, which not unlike the Old English wakes and the Ἀγάπαι of the early Christians, celebrates the foundation of the Church : —

"Early in the morning the Kirmse lads assemble together in their holiday clothes, and, accompanied by a band of music, go in procession to the village church, where the Pastor (who is indeed the Shepherd of his little flock) awaits their arrival, and delivers a short address or moral exhortation, appropriate to the occasion. After this the *Platz-Meister*, or director of the sports and pleasures, is chosen, who with his *Knecht*, or valet, and attendants, plays a conspicuous rôle. Having a branch of rosemary in one hand and a goblet in the other, which is from time to time replenished by the valet, the Platz-Meister proceeds to invite the principal persons of the village to the fête. On entering a house, he drains his cup to the health of its owner, and, in formal speech, invites him to the feast. He then *sur le champ* requests permission to dance with the gude man's wife, or should her dancing days be over (which, by the bye, is rarely the case), with the daughter. This is called the *Ehrentanz*, or dance of honor, and is never refused. In return for these civilities, the valet always receives a giant-sized cake, of which some hundreds are prepared the previous week, and which form the staple article of the evening's refreshment. The invitations being concluded, the dance is commenced under the Linden-tree ; but first by the youths alone, who dance the *Ronde*, after which they go in quest of their partners, having little gala wands in their hands. Naturally the maidens, nothing loth, are not unprepared, but attired in their best, and each having a *Schärpe* or scarf in her hand, await with anxious expectation the arrival of the swain, who, if he be fortunate enough to obtain the father's consent to taking out the lass as his partner for the day, attaches the scarf to her left shoulder in token of consent, while she in return adorns his hat with ribbons and with spangles. On her arrival she likewise must drink to the health of the assembled company. Then come the parents and the elders ; nor do they omit the pleasing task of quaffing the goblet in the cause of mirth and gayety. Now begins the dance in right earnest, the *Schleifer* and the *Hosper*, the Zweitritt and Schottish, and continues until six o'clock, when they join the festive board, and restore the system to its tone of vigour and hilarity. After that the dance is resumed, and with the aid of cake and beer, is prolonged, until midnight hours resign the merry troop to friendly Morpheus. The second day is a repetition of the first ; the third, however, is varied by the *Hammel Reiden* and the *Hahnenschlag*. The first is a horse-race, but derives its name from the circumstance of the prize being a fat sheep, which the winner obtains, and which being decked out with flowers and ribbons, is attached to the goal or winning-post. The second is the source of much amusement. Poor chanticleer, being placed under an inverted bowl, the youths, blindfold, successively try to release him by cracking his brittle gaol with sticks. This was a game very common both in England and France. 'Throwing at the Cock' on Shrove Tuesday. In France, the Gallorum Pugna is described in Carpentius Glossarium, A. D. 1458, Abbeville. 'Petierunt a magistro, Erardo Maquart magistro scholarum ejusdem villæ de Ramern, quatenus liberaret et traderet eis unum Gallum quam sicut dicebant idem magister scholarum delebat eis die ipsa (Carneprivii) ut jacerent baculos ad Gallum ipsum more solito pro earum exhileratione et ludo,' etc. On the fourth and last day, styled the *Bettel-Tag*, the young folks disguise themselves, and the people from the neighboring village likewise come in masquerade, dressed as Cossacks and Hussars, not forgetting the character of the *Hans Wurst*, or Jack Pudding. They go about requesting *salt* with true Etonian *nonchalance;* and the proceeds of the morning *recueil,* which are always donations in kind, furnish a far from despicable repast, which, after the usual quantum of dancing, drinking, smoking, and singing, winds up this national festivity."

INDEX.

www.ingramcontent.com/pod-product-compliance
Lightning Source LLC
Chambersburg PA
CBHW030346270326
41926CB00009B/975